ROCD

Is it a thing?

ROCD

Is it a thing?

Understanding & Overcoming Relationship OCD

TRACY FOSTER

Disclaimer

The information in this book is general guidance about the subject matter and not a specific person's individual circumstances. Neither is it a substitute for medical or alternative professional advice on specific or personal circumstances. Please consult with your medical practitioner or other health care professional if you are experiencing levels of distress that might require additional intervention. As far as the author is aware, the information given is accurate and up to date. The author does not assume responsibility for omissions, alternative interpretations or errors on the subject matter. The author disclaims, as far as UK law allows, any liability arising directly or indirectly from the use or misuse of the information contained in this publication.

First paperback edition [March 2023]

Book design by Publishing Push
Illustrations by Sarah Colbert

ISBNs
Paperback: 978-1-80227-985-6
eBook: 978-1-80227-986-3

Contents

List of Figures

Acknowledgements

To my wonderful family, who like the expression "there is a book in everyone." I finally found the book in me, so I value them all for listening to me and being supportive, encouraging, and motivational for quite some time while I've been putting this all together. The same goes for all my friends and Marja Coombes, my counselling supervisor. Thank you!

Special thanks to my oldest and dearest friend, Sarah Colbert (Senior Graphic Designer), for designing my illustrations. I'll do the words, and you do the creation! I value our friendship more than you can imagine.

Introduction

Relationship OCD: Is it a Thing?

This is the most frequently asked question, so if you're asking yourself this right now, you're questioning whether this is the right relationship for you or if this person is the right one. You're looking for 100% certainty.

Yes, it is 'a thing'.

What is going on in your mind, and what are you doing to recognise this as 'a thing'?

Relationship OCD (ROCD) is a sub-set of obsessive-compulsive disorder (OCD) and is highly distressing and confusing. It causes you to question, obsessively and in detail, whether your partner is right for you, whether you love them enough and whether they love you. It's challenging and overwhelming. ROCD can also leave you feeling very alone and isolated; many suffer in silence.

As in OCD, you're experiencing obsessive, intrusive thoughts and images and compulsive behaviours that are too difficult to resist. You're constantly searching for the answer to the anxiety-provoking relationship thought through rumination and compulsions.

Reassurance seeking and checking behaviours in ROCD can occur more subtly than visibly practical rituals (compulsions) like handwashing, counting and checking that the gas is off or doors are locked repeatedly. It might look like gaining comfort from friends and family by continually asking and questioning their thoughts about your relationship, studying your internal emotional states or heavily researching the internet for answers (research styles that include internet usage have recently been labelled *doom scrolling* when it's accompanied by high anxiety levels).

> *"Doomscrolling or doomsurfing is the act of spending excessive screen time devoted to the absorption of negative news. Increased consumption of predominantly negative news may result in harmful psychophysiological responses in some cases."*
> *– Wikipedia.*

Everyone I have worked with has agreed that after finding some initial information on OCD or ROCD, they end up on forum pages where others have the same, similar or other anxiety fuelled relationship thoughts. This ends with the ROCD sufferer potentially adding new thoughts to their list of things to check. Little knowledge is gained to decrease symptoms, but they find a whole load more to think about.

All the people I've supported with ROCD have encountered three common themes:

1. They experience high anxiety levels in other areas of their lives and relationships and refer to themselves as worriers or overthinkers.
2. They have previously had or currently experience OCD in other areas of their life – not necessarily by engaging in ritualistic behaviours like I previously mentioned, but more in obsessive, compulsive and intrusive thinking styles and reassurance/checking behaviours.

3. They experience low self-esteem, which impacts their self-worth. The person recognises that they often look for external validation from others or hold a perception of what they believe other people's expectations of them are. They frequently feel that they are 'not good enough'.

Considering these themes, you may not have recognised how maladaptive thinking can intrude into your relationship. Additionally, subconscious beliefs around relationships can occur for no apparent reason. I will explore and refer to this in later chapters.

If this sounds familiar, then you may also relate to some of the most common thinking patterns I've come across below:

- Believing your relationship will not work out based on uncertainty.
- Asking yourself if your partner is the right person for you.
- Checking for intelligence, appearance, social qualities, personality and achievement even when, objectively, you might deem these thoughts inappropriate or untrue at times. This causes you so much distress that it leads you to question your decision-making and whether you love your partner.
- Constantly seeking reassurance from others when something starts your nagging doubts.
- Comparing your relationship to your friends' or people you know – or don't know – on social platforms.
- Finding it challenging to control your thinking and avoiding situations where triggers may present themselves.
- Feeling guilty and ashamed about the way you think.
- Making lists of pros and cons about your relationship with your partner or your partner alone.

- Internally check and monitor your feelings for your partner at any moment.
- Consistently 'scanning' your internal physical sensations, looking for anxiety symptoms that could prove something wrong with your relationship.
- Looking for constant passion and the immense feelings of the 'honeymoon period' that lead to fairy-tale endings.
- Chasing intense feelings.
- Researching ROCD endlessly, finding similarities to others and becoming more confused.

Focusing on your relationship can be relentless, overwhelming, time-consuming and damaging. Establishing a relationship in the first place can be tough because you're not truly present in the 'getting to know each other' or foundation stages. You might be unable to move a relationship forward, or you may feel stuck when catastrophic consequences are inevitable after an ROCD thinking spree.

When you're constantly preoccupied with doubts, relationship satisfaction can be poor. Healthy and happy relationships can end when one partner continually analyses them, leaving the other partner angry or confused about the relentless questioning of their love and commitment to the relationship, reassurance seeking, avoidance and distancing behaviours.

Similarly, like anxiety and OCD, low self-worth and self-esteem can also unconsciously manifest themselves in relationships. This theme can sometimes feel more difficult to relate to as everyone can subconsciously hold on to internal beliefs about themselves, so they are outside their awareness. This means behaving or coping with thoughts and feelings in subconscious ways as well.

With clients, I work on introducing an understanding of cognitive behaviour therapy (CBT) with ROCD. It serves to bring awareness to these subconscious thoughts that may not have been apparent.

If you feel unsure whether your self-esteem and self-worth are entangled with your relationship, you might want to consider these questions:

- Do you feel better about yourself when your relationship feels like it's going well, and you feel in harmony?
- If you have a disagreement or difference of opinion, does that affect how you feel about yourself in general?
- If people make positive remarks about you and your relationship, does that make you feel better?

If this sounds like you so far, this book is for you. I have a favourite exercise for you to carry out to establish a sense of identity that you will love.

In my earlier years of working and researching ROCD, as I mentioned previously, I recognised three presenting themes that can occur outside of your relationship and in it: *Anxiety* and *OCD*, which may or may not have been diagnosed by your GP or other mental health care provider, and *self-esteem/self-worth*.

We'll look at each of these later on.

My research and experience working with OCD have also identified stereotypical ideas about what OCD is, and why it's a constant minefield to navigate.

You might have been in contact with friends, family and social circles where people say things like, "Oh, I'm so OCD," when, really, they mean they prefer having their baked beans or tinned tomatoes lined up neatly in their kitchen cupboards.

Mostly, people have ways they like things to be, such as habits and preferences. Therefore, it's worth noting that if somebody truly experiences OCD, they feel tremendous emotional distress if some of these things don't work out correctly or they don't feel 100% certain. As a result, their anxiety can go through the roof.

When people start their ROCD journey, many often roll their eyes and nod their heads in recognition of these themes. Not all people, of course. OCD has many facets, and everyone is individual in terms of why it presents itself in their lives as it does and its origins.

This book explores OCD/intrusive and distressing thoughts (specifically regarding relationships), the accompanying compulsions and how to overcome them. It will support you in moving away from rumination (focusing on thoughts and feelings) and towards personal goals and outcomes. That's not to say you won't discover a new sense of self and improvements that you like in other areas of your life, however.

Additionally, it's not designed to save deteriorating relationships when signals indicate an unsuitable connection due to a lack of consistent real value.

Later in this book, completing the **Core Values exercise** will support you in working towards a positive sense of worth and self-esteem.

If you're also engaging in personal therapy and experience uncomfortable levels of distress that might come to light from other unresolved issues, discuss and explore this with your therapist, as they may be able to signpost you to additional support or different resources. The same applies if you're utilising self-help guides such as this. If your general mental health is being severely impacted, don't hesitate to contact your GP or mental health provider.

Background

I am a qualified integrative humanistic counsellor and cognitive behavioural therapist registered with the British Association for Counselling & Psychotherapy (BACP). My passion for and commitment to this anxiety-provoking, debilitating condition called **relationship obsessive-compulsive disorder (ROCD)** helped me to develop my research to support and improve my work. If you want to overcome your ROCD, this book can help you.

It's written with you in mind and includes education and guided self-help techniques based on my knowledge and understanding of genuine issues clients have explored with me.

Previous clients have been a primary resource in guiding my research. All of my clients' experiences have given me helpful insight into the education and support I have offered for clients resolving their ROCD and finding peace in their relationships.

When you're not experiencing a cycle of ROCD, I suspect you can rationally say your relationship is great, fantastic, he/she/they are unique, and loads of other positive attributes you can care to mention.

Isn't that what makes it so very hard?

Have you tried explaining that to anyone in the hope they understand and, at best, anyone you speak to about it usually says something like, 'listen to your gut' or, 'if you think it's wrong, then it probably is'.

In the initial sections, I will explain what OCD is. I will describe the concept of cognitive behavioural therapy (CBT) and how to use it yourself. I will also explore how ROCD can stem from internal belief systems. This will help you recognise how you think about your relationship and the certainty and guarantees you are looking for. Think of it not as trying to resolve actual problems within the relationship but more about working through how you think about it.

You'll learn how to influence your own life.

It might seem a little boring to elaborate on certain things, but I believe it's helpful to understand what's going on and make some sense of it based on a bit of knowledge and know-how.

Many psychological approaches can draw upon these theories for other problems as well. The focus of this book is to help you further your self-awareness towards romantic relationships. That's not to say it won't also impact other areas of your life. You can expand your knowledge with further reading of the reference material supplied at the back of the book if you wish.

My professional training and experience come from my time as an integrative humanistic counsellor. This approach considers you as the whole person you are and uses cognitive behavioural approaches to support you in challenging and changing negative thoughts and behaviours.

By understanding OCD and how it can find a channel into your relationships, you will be able to identify relationship OCD more clearly and recognise it as a sub-set of OCD. OCD can find a way into anything, especially if it's something you value and care for.

Other helpful resources from my experience include mindfulness techniques, my studies as a life coach and my knowledge and understanding of working with exposure and response therapy. Many therapists and mental health organisations consider this the gold standard for overcoming OCD. Yes, it can be overcome.

Based on all these techniques, I have put together a set of practical tasks for you.

All of them are put into manageable sections and explained, so you can easily understand what to do and why it's helpful, and you will be able to measure your improvement. They're designed to help you face your relationship fears and tolerate the anxiety from your obsessive thinking from a renewed perspective. You can go back to the tasks and update your ideas if you want to as you work on your new sense of self. Each exercise is explained individually, although they are all interlinked, so I've indicated where you might want to refer to another activity in some areas to help you.

It's entirely up to you how you use this book, but you might find it helpful to read the main information in each chapter and then revisit the activities and exercises afterwards.

I also suggest that you get yourself a journal to record the activities and exercises, so that you can reflect on, update and monitor your progress.

Take this work from the standpoint that there is only one you – your unique and individual self.

If you're wondering why and how I got into working with ROCD, here's some background information on where it all began:

Over ten years ago, a client contacted me with an accompanying magazine article outlining ROCD symptoms and said, "Can you help me?" I wasn't familiar with this condition, but I said, with my counselling hat on, "I can support you with how you feel and explore your thinking. Shall we go from there?"

We worked together for an extended period, in detail, about many things. I'm not suggesting it will take you a long time. The work with this particular client took a while because we covered many things, which I have now condensed into a concise, usable format, and much has been included over the years.

Since that day, I have supported hundreds of people worldwide in understanding relationship OCD and overcoming it.

Some positive feedback

Here are a few comments from previous clients, shared with their permission, regarding what has been particularly helpful for them:

"Using the CBT blueprint in 'real-time' has helped me improve coping strategies that previously didn't correspond with my feelings or thoughts".

"I like parts of myself which I could never have imagined".

"I'm not seeing superficial things as problems now".

"I'm seeing the thoughts as the problem, not the relationship".

"I'm looking at the value my relationship brings to my life".

"I want to thank you… I don't know where I'd be or what I'd have done without our sessions over the last few months. Although it was a hard time for me, you made it feel like a positive experience, as now I know how much therapy can help me and can help other people, and before, I didn't think it would help at all. I also now know how to rationalise my thoughts and that all thoughts aren't real, which has helped my ROCD, and I have even used some of the techniques you have taught me to help with my health anxiety. I was on a plane yesterday (the thing I'm most scared of EVER, haha) and managed to remain calm and think of my internal bodyguard… I've felt hardly any anxiety since our last session,

and even before that, I was feeling less and less anxious with the methods you have taught me, so thank you!"

"The flexibility scale helped me when making decisions was too stressful because I wanted it to be the 'perfect' choice, and it helps with perfectionism and a rigid mindset in general".

"I found the skill of looking at the 'what if?' questions and turning them into 'if…' also helpful, which I think helps take away some of the urgency in anxiety".

"One of the key things that helped me was looking at relationship misconceptions. Social media gives us a pretty unhealthy idea of what a relationship 'should' look like, and that's accepted as the norm and can be triggering because real life isn't like that".

"Realising that its ok to feel unattracted to your partner sometimes, or that we all go through times where we don't feel love for our partners, helped me to feel more 'normal' and like I didn't need to end my relationship because of these things".

"I was surprised, but having more compassion for myself helped so much. Any time these thoughts cropped up, I'd be so harsh with myself, which compounded the issue. Speaking more kindly to myself brought down that horrible sense of danger I felt".

I hope this fills you with optimism to start your journey, knowing that you can equally take some positives from this book.

OCD is stubborn, as you know, so consistently using some or all the activities and exercises suggested will be helpful.

Don't forget your journal.

CHAPTER 1

Obsessive-Compulsive Disorder (OCD)

Did you know? ⟡

OCD-UK states that three-quarters of a million people live with OCD, affecting all ages, genders and social/cultural backgrounds.

Through evidenced studies by researchers and mental health clinicians worldwide, the *Diagnostic and Statistical Manual of Mental Disorders (DSM-5)*, used by clinicians to diagnose mental health conditions, now provides OCD with a stand-alone category as a debilitating condition, rather than its previous sub-category under anxiety disorders, even though sufferers of OCD experience high levels of anxiety.

The *World Health Organization (WHO)* ranks OCD as *"amongst the top ten most disabling illnesses by lost income and decreased quality of life."*

Historical Background

OCD-UK's research shows that OCD dates to the 1400s, described mainly as being about obsessive fears around religion – commonly known as "scrupulosity" – and suffering doubts of sin and sinful thoughts.

This theory evolved in the 1700s and 1800s when physicians implied there were more neuropathological conditions. A French psychiatrist, Jean-Étienne-Dominique Esquirol (1772–1840), described OCD as monomania or partial insanity. Several French psychiatrists had the same ideas and felt that OCD was also linked to a lack of control of the mind. Even during the 19th and 20th centuries, OCD was considered a degenerative disorder of the brain, which only encouraged the stigma of mental illness, leaving OCD the secret illness.

The 19th century and early 20th century works by French psychologist Pierre Janet (1859–1947) and – a name you may be more familiar with – the Austrian founder of psychoanalysis, Sigmund Freud (1856-1939), linked subconscious and conscious conflicts in the mind that lead OCD sufferers to carry out specific actions, which only serve to provide temporary relief from the anxiety of their thoughts. Inspired by his case study called *"Rat Man"*, Freud's concept was that the OCD sufferer developed compulsions to dilute the obsessive ideas.

It wasn't until the early 1970s that cognitive behavioural therapies, exposure and response therapy, acceptance and commitment therapy and mindfulness-based techniques proved to be more effective and replaced the more Freudian psychoanalysis work, which has proven to be more effective. Some methods are included in this guide that you can try as alternatives to your current coping strategies, which, as you have already experienced, do not work (or do not work for long).

Although it remains unknown exactly what causes OCD, research suggests several components, such as biological makeup, genetics and people's environments.

OCD sufferers commonly have excessive thoughts, which lead to compulsive behaviours. These thoughts are not your daily worries. They can be persistent, intrusive and unwanted. OCD sufferers experience significant distress and anxiety due to the perceived meaning of these thoughts and the high importance placed upon them. The compulsions are designed to rid the person of the thoughts or check out their validity to find certainty, guarantees and conclusions and to reduce anxiety.

It is, unfortunately, common in our modern-day language to say "I/he/she/they are *so* OCD," when what is meant is that they have a preference. You can probably relate it to someone you know if you're reading this.

Other common disorders related to OCD can take the form of or be found alongside:

- Religious rituals
- Superstitions
- Hoarding
- Eating disorders
- Drug and alcohol misuse
- Body dysmorphic disorder
- Health anxiety
- Trichotillomania
- Tics
- Tourette's syndrome
- Morbid jealousy

Depending on the situation, you can see how many obsessive thoughts, obsessions or rituals are used.

OCD is also not particular to anyone specifically. Here are some famous people that are OCD sufferers. They're all from different backgrounds, as stated by *The Mayo Clinic* in the USA and *The Journal of Advanced Practice Nursing (2016)*:

- Daniel Radcliffe
- Howard Stern

- David Beckham
- Katy Perry
- Justin Timberlake
- Howie Mandel
- Charlize Theron
- Leonardo Dicaprio
- Lena Dunham
- Fiona Apple
- Donald Trump
- Cameron Diaz
- Charles Dickens
- Woody Allen
- Paul Gascoigne
- Jeremy Kyle
- Harrison Ford
- Steven Gerrard
- Albert Einstein
- Charles Darwin
- Michelangelo
- Beethoven

That's a little background history and understanding of OCD, which you might find helpful. Of course, there are plenty of professional reference guides for further and more profound knowledge of OCD for all the above issues.

OCD leaves you feeling out of control with your intrusive, worrying thoughts. The images of the thought content play out in your mind, like a film reel on a loop, which instils severe anxiety and fear. The sense you make of them is equally disturbing, leaving you questioning your integrity and feeling like you'll carry out some heinous crime, following through with hurting someone or yourself.

Further probing results in rumination over the past. This leads to those 'what if' questions based on future speculation. You go round and round in circles. Intrusive thoughts are repetitive, and your coping strategies are compulsions to counteract or neutralise the thoughts and relieve your anxiety.

Relationship OCD sufferers search for the 'perfect relationship', and the obsessive thoughts and compulsions reflect this.

"OCD can be overcome, and you are not becoming crazy."

(Veale & Willson, 2009. Overcoming Obsessive Compulsive Disorder)

CHAPTER 2

Cognitive Behaviour Therapy

Historical Background

American psychiatrist Aaron T. Beck (1921–2021) is regarded as the founder of cognitive behaviour therapy (CBT), based on the groundwork of psychologist Albert Ellis (1913-2007). His key ideas originated initially from working with depressed patients who experienced many negative thoughts (cognitions) from interpretations about themselves, their environment/the world around them and the future. They determined that patients commonly overestimated the negative consequences and outcomes of not getting something right or perfect.

In medical terms, 'cognition' is connected to mental processes through thinking, relating to, reasoning, remembering, imagining, learning and judging *(Cambridge Dictionary)*.

Therapists today recognise that these thinking errors are common in OCD, leading to obsessions and compulsions.

What is it?

The theory behind CBT is that if we relate negative thoughts to specific situations, they form a vicious cycle that links negative feelings, physical symptoms and behaviours. CBT aims to examine and challenge these subconscious thoughts attached to current situations, improve feelings and explore and develop coping strategies that are more effective for problem-solving.

When I trained as a cognitive behaviour therapist, I understood this as a subconscious 'blueprint' in our mind (see diagram below). Many variations of the CBT model similarly demonstrate this, which you may have come across.

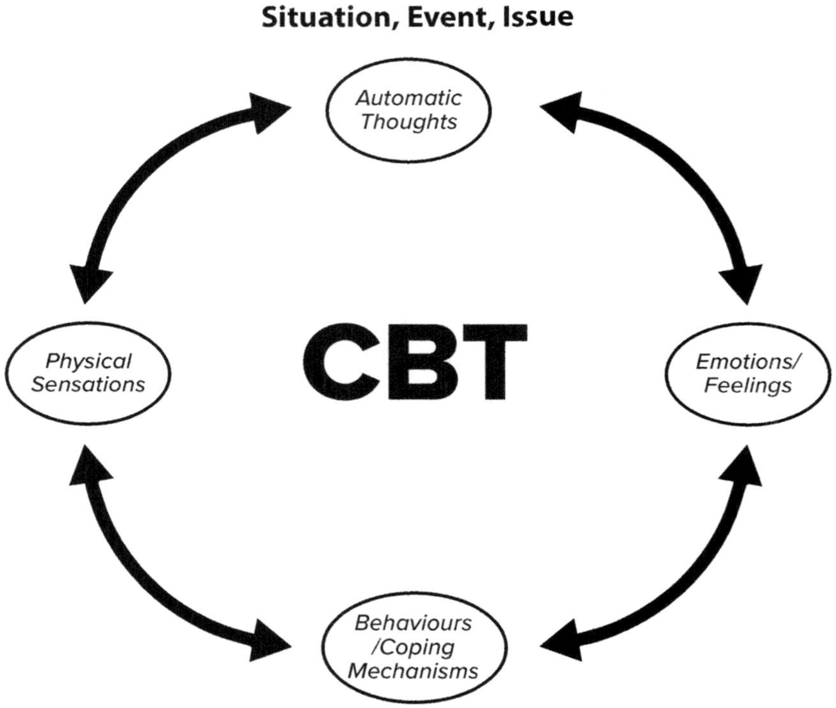

Situation, Event, Issue

Figure 1 – CBT Subconscious Blueprint

I use the concept of CBT not only as a way to deepen self-awareness but also as a valuable tool to help you map your present moments mindfully – what your actions or coping mechanisms are likely to be when you think and feel as you do, including your physical response, which, within your ROCD symptoms, is often experienced as anxiety.

CBT is widely used to treat many mental health conditions, including anxiety, depression, eating disorders, bipolar disorder, borderline personality disorder, phobias, panic disorder, OCD and PTSD. It can also be used for some long-term health conditions.

How it works

CBT is designed to help you break down these four linked components (automatic subconscious thoughts, feelings/emotions, coping strategies and physical symptoms) in more manageable and positive ways. It can help you explore subconscious negative core beliefs you hold about yourself, understand their origins and challenge their validity. By referring to this blueprint, you can recognise further negative thoughts and feelings that keep you trapped in vicious cycles.

CBT is a helpful starting point, as it helps you deal with your presenting problem, for example, your ROCD.

CBT commonly includes exercises outside the therapy room, so it takes some commitment to add routine and structure to your day to carry out the suggested tasks.

I feel it's beneficial to carry out the tasks suggested by your therapist (and within this self-help guide) in structured ways. They will help you further your self-awareness and bring attention to the cycles of thoughts, feelings, behaviours and physical symptoms. This will enable you to slow your thinking down to gain perspective and make more helpful autonomous decisions for yourself.

The suggestions I include within this book outline some coping mechanisms or behaviours you can try, which are not exhaustive.

However, used consistently with personalised tweaks if required, they can offer a good deal of relief in handling overthinking and intrusive thoughts, not just in your relationship but in other areas of your life too.

When clients engage in ROCD therapy, I explain CBT and how everyone forms subconscious core beliefs about themselves by recounting some of their life experiences, going back to childhood and earlier interpretations.

This helps people determine thoughts they've had about themselves at a deeper level, the feelings that come up for them and where this evidence came from.

An important feature of CBT often depends on a particular style of dialogue between therapist and client called *Socratic questioning.* This means using *open-ended questions* to encourage this deeper level of awareness. It offers the client insight into the origins of their beliefs and values and how they affect how they think and feel now – information previously held outside of their attention.

Did you know?

The phrase *Socratic questioning* comes from the ancient Greek philosopher Socrates (c.470BCE-399BCE), who set the foundations for western understanding of logic and philosophy and was further demonstrated by his famously known students Plato (c.424/423BCE) and Aristotle (384BCE-322BCE).

This style of explorative thinking challenges assumptions made and explores the evidence. It provides an opportunity to evaluate different viewpoints and consider the validity of these deeply held views in the present day.

Open-ended questions start with *what, where, how, when* and *why*. Questions in this style will likely open a more detailed and descriptive response. I use the 'why' question sparingly because if we could all answer the 'why' so quickly, we would all have the answer.

Below is an explanation of how the CBT model works:

Triggers

Triggers refer to the situation, event or issue.

If you refer to Figure 1 – CBT Subconscious Blueprint, you will see the heading *situation, event or issue.* These trigger the cycle of the four linked components in subconscious ways, and are, therefore, outside of your awareness. Four common core beliefs (automatic thoughts) have been identified, which are explained below.

Automatic Thoughts

The four identified core beliefs within CBT, through this style of Socratic questioning, are usually:

- People don't or won't like me
- I'm a failure
- I'm not worthy / I'm worthless
- I'm not enough / I'm not good enough

These core beliefs form as truths in your mind as subconsciously you collect 'evidence' that supports them over time and from any situation.

Feelings/Emotions

Considering these beliefs in conjunction with Figure 1 of the CBT template, the accompanying feelings and emotions are unlikely to be positive. These automatic thoughts could be accompanied by feelings of sadness, upset, despair, anger, hopelessness, helplessness, frustration, anger, jealousy, envy, guilt and shame. You may identify with some of these and have some of your own to add. Guilt, shame and embarrassment often feature as negative feelings for ROCD sufferers, so I've added some information on these feelings towards the end of the book.

It makes sense, then, that if you experience a negative thought about yourself, a negative feeling or emotion won't be far behind, nor will how you cope or behave with it.

Coping Mechanisms/Behaviours

Some common coping mechanisms and behaviours within ROCD (which we'd call *compulsions*) are:

- **Checking behaviours**
  This can be your internal feelings, checking out with other people or checking your partner for clues or evidence. This checking style can include all kinds of things ranging from levels of attractiveness and personality, as I mentioned before, to the minutest detail, which is incredibly important to you. It could be down to how their ears have aligned on either side of their head, the size of their eyes, whether their features are too close or too wide, the size and shape of their nose, the colour of their eyebrows, a distinguishing mark on their face such as a mole, an irritating laugh or specific phrases they might say in front of particular friends or in social situations where you check to see if they've embarrassed you. Or maybe you're doing personality tests on social media or checking your and your partner's horoscopes.

- **Reassurance seeking**

  You seek reassurance from other people (friends, family, your partner) and high-level internet searching, hoping to gain approval (which can affect your self-esteem and self-worth).

- **Avoidance/withdrawal**
  - Not spending time with your partner for fear of being triggered by anxious thoughts.
  - Not attending that social gathering you were invited to so that others won't see how bad or wrong your relationship is.
  - The reluctance of conversations that include moving your relationship forward.
  - Avoiding perceived happier couples.
  - Avoidance of discussions around other people's breakups or even obsessively wanting to know all the details to compare their relationship to your own.
  - Withdrawing of affection in your relationship, including sex.

- **Comparing**
  - Comparison of others' relationships to your own – good or bad.
  - Comparison of your past relationships with finite details.
  - Writing out endless pros and cons lists.
  - Assigning deep meaning to social media quotes about relationships.
  - Scrutinising your friends' social media posts or photos that look more favourable than your own (this can also affect your self-esteem and self-worth).

- **People-pleasing / approval seeking**
  - Putting additional or unwanted pressure on yourself to say "yes" to your internal 'shoulds' that are connected

to your relationship beliefs and requirements, of which there can be a long list.

We'll look at these separately, as they can be held as subconscious beliefs, built up and stored over time in your mind's 'relationships filing cabinet' (also affecting your self-esteem and self-worth).

Within ROCD, due to the personal nature of our intimate relationships, these *automatic thoughts* (core beliefs) attach themselves to the couple in the relationship, as they're often a reflection of how you feel about yourself:

- People won't like us as a couple.
- Our relationship is a failure, or it won't last.
- Our relationship is worthless.
- Our relationship isn't good enough.

I'm using this blueprint as an example for ROCD. Therefore, on deeper exploration, you may feel like this in other areas of your life when triggered by core beliefs.

Example early exercise:

- Draw your own CBT template based on Figure 1.
- At the top, write down a situation you might find yourself in that triggers your ROCD.
- In the 'automatic thoughts' box, write a few thoughts and consider how you believe these thoughts to be true.
- You might think about your ideas around relationships, where the influence and opinion came from and what this means for you. Use open-ended Socratic questions to guide

you, e.g. "When have I felt like that in the past?" and "What's happened for me to feel or believe this is true?"

- In the 'feelings/emotions' box, write a few feelings you might experience. Note: anxiety isn't a *feeling* per se, even though we often say we 'feel anxious'. It's a physical response to your feelings, so anxiety goes in the physical symptoms box if that's the response you experience.

Lastly, write what you'll do as an action in the 'coping strategies/ behaviours' box. What do you notice? This is just a taster exercise, and we'll revisit it in later chapters so that you can use it as a real-time mapping process in some of the additional activities.

"We are all influenced by current trends in what we see as important."

– (Veale & Willson, 2009. Overcoming Obsessive Compulsive Disorder).

CHAPTER 3

Relationship OCD

Professor Paul Salkovkis, Professor of Clinical Psychology & Applied Science at the Institute of Psychiatry at King's College in London, authenticates the work of the authors David Veale and Rob Willson, consultant psychiatrists and CBT therapists, in their book *Overcoming Obsessive Compulsive Disorder*, which I've found to be a valuable resource throughout my OCD research. They state:

> *"...the form of OCD may differ from one culture to another. This is because the content of an obsession is usually what a person does not want to think or a kind of harm they particularly want to prevent. We are all influenced by current trends in what we see as important".*

OCD can be a combination of genetics (therefore anxiety susceptibility), and psychological and social factors. We can conclude that obsessive thoughts around relationships can be prevalent when considering the modern-day trend of having 'essential elements to consider' within relationships.

Considering current trends, with the influence of social media at an all-time high, expectations and comparisons within relationships

17

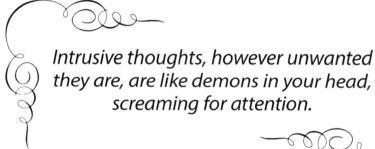

Intrusive thoughts, however unwanted they are, are like demons in your head, screaming for attention.

are elevated. My usual client age range for experiencing ROCD symptoms and high-end users of social platforms is generally between the ages of 18 and 35, with the age range of users across most social platforms being between 16 and 34, according to research carried out by *Ofcom* in 2020 across two groups.

The Gottman Institute state in their findings that, *"In 2019, the average person spent 144 minutes per day on social media,"* (Clement 2020) and went on to say, *according to Media Dependency Theory, the higher the dependence a person has on media, the stronger the influence on an individual's perceptions and behaviours," (Joo & Teng, 2017, p.36).*

Therefore, social media can play a big part in people's perceptions, comparisons, and ideals in their relationships, causing obsessive thinking about socially acceptable relationship goals.

In chapter 6, **Subconscious Relationship Beliefs and Requirements**, and its accompanying exercise, I'll add some further findings from *The Gottman Institute* research, highlighting the negative impact of comparisons in relationships when you already harbour ideals that are outside of your awareness. The exercise will enable you to consider your influences.

3.1 Obsessive thoughts and compulsions in ROCD

Out of the blue, an obsessive thought (like one of the examples I gave earlier) comes into your head that you don't want. It's intrusive, causes distress and anxiety, and you just can't rid yourself of it.

The emotional distress this causes can be immense, and for you experiencing it, it's difficult to leave alone. Hence, it's essential to pay the thought much attention and search for its meaning. Surely, it must be TRUE if you thought it. Something MUST be wrong. Something WILL inevitably go wrong if you don't find the answer!

Initially, you may push it away only to find the intrusive thought returns with a greater sense of urgency in needing an answer. This leads to increased anxiety. It's like a demon in your head screaming for attention.

Quite often in ROCD, you feel tremendously responsible for this thinking style, which causes alarm, fear, frustration, guilt and shame, to name just a few emotions. Consequently, you'll try to search for the answer and the truth. These thoughts create a roadmap for other ideas, causing more emotional distress and a potentially unrealistic need for certainty.

This diagram shows how you can get caught up in an *emotional washing machine*, where any realistic, rational or objective thoughts have gone out of the window, leading to compulsive behaviours (not dissimilar to Fig 1 – CBT Blueprint).

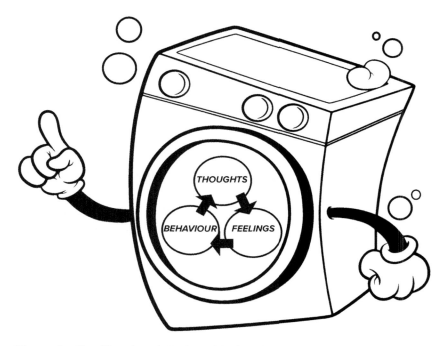

Figure 2 – The 'Emotional Washing Machine'

I describe it as an emotional washing machine so you can visualise how fast and furious these thoughts become. One thought causes a negative feeling, which reinforces the thought, which leads to the feeling or emotion being intensified, which further brings about another negative, uncertain thought that re-intensifies the emotion, and so on. When your washing machine starts up, you can see your laundry tumbling around, and as the washing cycle continues, it eventually reaches a spin cycle; you can't see your clothing during this time. This is similar to losing sight of any rational, realistic or objective thoughts – just as your clothing is stuck to the sides of the drum during the spin cycle, your thoughts get stuck in a process. (Chapter 8, **Fact or Opinion?**, discusses this a little more, with a practical exercise to work on after considering some anxiety self-management techniques).

The need for certainty brings a sense of urgency, leading to excessive reassurance seeking and checking behaviours. You might seek this reassurance by asking other people, such as friends and family, or researching incessantly through the internet or other resources. You might check the internal state of how you feel at any given moment to reduce the anxiety that starts to feel intolerable. As you can see from the *emotional washing machine* diagram, the one thing that doesn't happen is 'reduced anxiety'. These excessive reassurances and checking behaviours are referred to as *compulsions*.

Obsessions = thoughts

You might check in with yourself to see if the anxiety about your relationship has gone away. You've just re-engaged with and applied meaning to your thoughts when you do that. Another series of thoughts occurs, or the older thoughts resurface.

Behaviours or coping strategies = compulsions (the actions you take to reduce or rid yourself of the anxiety).

Your compulsions increase because of the meaning you apply to your thoughts – frequently, that they must be true if you've thought of them, and you can't tolerate the uncertainty of not knowing.

The trouble with relationship OCD thoughts is that many of them probably start with 'what if...', 'this means...', 'this could mean...', 'maybe...' and 'might...'. Unfortunately, those thoughts become absolutes in your mind and are often planted in the future.

One common compulsion is checking with and getting reassurance from your friends and loved ones about your concerns. You may do this several times, and the friend or loved one – with your best interests at heart and with their best intentions – may well advise you to listen to your gut instinct and suggest that, because of the frequency of your thoughts, they may well indicate real problems in your relationship. This reinforces your negative thought patterns and perpetuates your anxiety further because you feel they either don't understand what you're trying to explain, or it becomes a form of reassurance that your obsessive thoughts are true.

The anxiety is so great because your thoughts, when in an ROCD cycle, rarely match a rational, objective thinking cycle with the reality of your relationship, i.e. what you have evidenced in positive and valuable ways. They don't correspond, which causes so much anxiety/emotional distress and chaos in your life.

Many sources suggest that the human mind has literally thousands of thoughts per day. Working on the basis that we think day and night (unless we're in a deep sleep), many of them come from the environment around us in conscious ways, and others come from our interpretations of ourselves and our world subconsciously. Either way, we can potentially pick and choose the ones that hold some relevance because they're important and meaningful to us.

In chapter 7, **Managing Anxiety with ROCD**, I've selected mindfulness techniques to help manage these thoughts more effectively. You can integrate more mindfulness into your daily life to encourage a good sense of mental health and well-being.

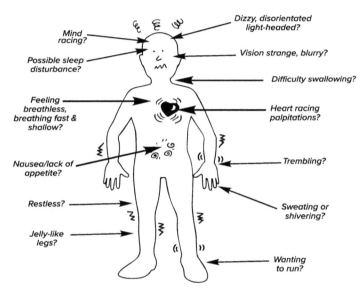

Figure 3 – Anxiety Symptoms

CHAPTER 4

Anxiety

What is it?

It's entirely natural to feel anxious from time to time. It's your body's immediate biological response to what you perceive as dangerous, unsafe, uncertain and unpredictable in some situations.

It's your body's primitive survival technique to help you deal with unexpected or life-threatening dangers. It's been around for millions of years and indicates that you need to do something rapidly to protect yourself.

As the more 'sophisticated' human beings we are today, we're not usually exploited or at risk of getting eaten by dangerous prehistoric animals as we were in the past; however, our DNA hasn't changed too much.

Anxiety is commonly known as your *fight or flight* response, and it's still needed for survival. Your mind signals to your other internal organs to be prepared by releasing adrenaline and noradrenaline hormones, which increase your breathing and pump up your heartbeat in readiness for this rapid reaction.

Physical symptoms can often include dizziness, headaches, tummy sensations (butterflies), needing to go to the toilet, sweaty hands, dry mouth, nausea, wobbly legs and palpitations. You might notice some or all of these symptoms. They feel uncomfortable and cause worry, so it's helpful to identify the physical symptoms you experience yourself.

In addition to the fight or flight response, physiologists now include *freeze and fawn* as a response in more modern times. A freeze response is what the name suggests – freeze or do nothing. The lesser-mentioned fawn response relates to pleasing or fawning, a coping mechanism for a potential fear of conflict or confrontation.

Do you recognise this lesser-known fawning or pleasing coping strategy in your relationship – or in other areas of your life – to avoid potential conflict or confrontation? This could be because your self-esteem has taken a hit and knocked down your self-worth!

Not many of us like conflict or confrontation, so it's easy to see how our anxiety levels can spike in certain situations, depending on how you view it.

Anxiety isn't dangerous, although intense anxiety can be very unpleasant. Still, it can keep you motivated and focused on doing your best and moving forwards positively, like taking exams or your driving test. It's a natural persuader to help you achieve positive outcomes. However, anxiety can feel constant and overwhelming for some people and can be detrimental to daily life, especially if it's out of proportion to the event itself.

Anxiety can be expected concerning many modern-day situations, such as financial worries and up-and-coming events or stress-related issues at work, school, home, and personal relationships. It can also be attributed to traumatic life situations and mefdical conditions, so it's always worth getting checked out by your medical professional if you have persistent concerns.

Anxiety symptoms that accompany your thoughts around your relationship negatively impact your general well-being, challenge your relationship and hamper its growth.

Chapter 7, **Managing Anxiety with ROCD**, will support you with strategies to manage anxiety effectively.

Another concept to bear in mind is that many ROCD sufferers use the intensity of their anxiety symptoms as a gauge or measuring stick that guides how valid they think their relationship thoughts are.

When you're in a spiral of ROCD thoughts, your anxiety increases, so using anxiety as a guide is unhelpful. The work I'll explore with you later relating to core values will help you establish a healthier, more authentic sense of self (your self-worth) that you like, enabling you to love yourself for the individual you are. This will provide a more effective measuring tool for managing your thoughts. Your core values will help you to problem-solve when negative emotions attached to adverse situations hit your self-esteem. These negative emotions or feelings don't accurately describe your character or personality. You can read more in chapter 5, **Self-Worth and Self-Esteem,** to understand the difference between the two.

If you also engage in personal therapy for ROCD, your therapist might have explored anxious attachment styles with you. It's helpful to look back on your relationship with your parents or primary caregivers if love, care and nurturing were inconsistent; it might – in part – help you make sense of why you question the security, safety and trust within your relationship that can lead to seeking constant reassurance and doubting your worth. People who've experienced consistent love, care and safety will develop a secure attachment style. There's some information on attachment styles within chapter 6, **Subconscious Relationship Beliefs and Requirements**.

Did you know? ☀

American physiologist, Walter Cannon, coined the phrase "fight or flight response" in the 1920s after he recognised the chain of reactions that the human body went through when dealing with threatening or potentially threatening situations.

Chapter 5

Self-worth and Self-esteem

Many people with ROCD symptoms don't always recognise that their self-worth or self-esteem can impact how they view their relationships, as interpretations can come from a subconscious place. Therefore, they are outside of your awareness. This, in part, is why I use the cognitive behaviour concept, initially to help you build a deeper knowledge of yourself so that you can further understand how you feel based on your interpretations from previous life experiences.

Self-worth and self-esteem are not the same, although they're related.

5.1 Self-worth

Self-worth forms the core beliefs you hold about yourself. If you experience low self-worth, you have negative judgements of your value and experience beliefs of 'not being good enough' and believe that others' views and opinions are more important than yours. These interpretations can show up in many situations and have a lasting impact on your strategies to cope with the thoughts, feelings and emotions you experience. Look back at chapter 2, **Cognitive Behaviour Therapy (CBT)** and Fig 1 – CBT Blueprint, to see how the relentless cycle of negative core beliefs is maintained and how it's become so natural to you that you don't even recognise it. It can form a misrepresentation of your whole self.

Building a good sense of self-worth is about accepting who you are and not judging yourself by what you have. Chapter 9, **Core Values**, will explain how you can build a realistic self-identity that YOU like and love (this is my favourite practical task because it can have a prolific effect on you and forms a central part of all the other activities). It's your guideline for living your REAL life. I always get excited about this part of supporting you with ROCD. I firmly believe it plays an integral role in overcoming poor self-worth because it works not only with your ROCD symptoms but the WHOLE YOU!

5.2 Self-esteem

Self-esteem is more subjective and applies more to your thoughts 'in the moment' when you're considering how 'good' you are or have been in certain situations. Therefore, you can judge yourself through the lens of negative thoughts about your worth and the feelings they generate. If you hold poor self-esteem, your thoughts more than likely lead to overthinking, which causes catastrophic outcomes and a lack of confidence.

This is where working on core values will also help you lessen the destructive negative thinking patterns of 'I always fail,' 'I always do this,' 'My relationships will always be like this' and 'I will never achieve…'. You can shift your thinking back to a healthier level of self-worth by using strategies to develop a more positive mindset and lessen extreme thinking, You will recognise this thinking as something you're experiencing at that moment rather than experiencing the thoughts as something that defines you. Using your healthy core values, including self-compassion balanced with personal boundaries within your self-worth, will provide you with healthier self-esteem.

CHAPTER 6

Subconscious Relationship Beliefs and Requirements

Where do they come from?

I'll explain these areas in more detail based on research from my client experiences.

6.1 Childhood Perceptions of Parents/Caregivers

As a young child, you initially learn about relationships from your parents or caregivers. These are your earliest memories for building a *relationship folder* in your mind to start collecting evidence and interpreting the meaning of that evidence. These interpretations and memories often inform your role in your adult relationships in the future.

You can't help being influenced by your life events. For example, you may have experienced your parents getting divorced and all the unhappiness and upset that may have caused. You might formulate a meaning that partners can't be trusted, relationships are unsafe and love is uncertain or conditional. You might interpret this as your rule to get it right in future relationships.

From previous clients' perspectives, expectations in relationships may be communicated explicitly to the other person in the hope that

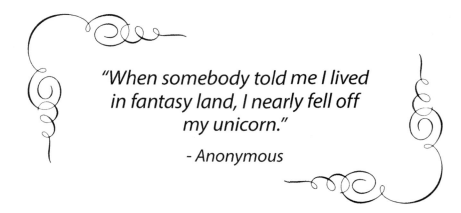

"When somebody told me I lived in fantasy land, I nearly fell off my unicorn."

- Anonymous

they'll be fulfilled or unsaid but still hoped for in *the longing that those expectations may be fulfilled.*

Michal Einav, clinical psychologist, specialist and senior lecturer in psychology at the *School of Behavioural Sciences,* has extensive experience in family dynamics and parent-child relationships and has carried out considerable research with psychodiagnostic assessments, focusing on the impact of these relationships.

Specifically, Einav's (2014) research in *'Perception About Parents' Relationship and Parenting Quality, Attachment Styles, and Young Adults' Intimate Expectations: A Cluster Analytic Approach, (July 2014)* states: *"Other expectations, equally influential, as to the explicit, are more implicit and may reflect the individuals' unconscious attempt to fulfil personal, sometimes childhood needs through the relationship. Often, people expect their spouse to compensate for qualities and characteristics they lack to provide specific experiences such as nurturing or security that they have received in insufficient quantity or quality." (Knee & Canevello, 2006).*

This makes sense if you're hoping to fulfil unmet needs through your relationships, which can increase the responsibility you might put on yourself and the other person to meet those needs. It can lead to co-dependency in adult relationships.

6.2 Fairy Tales and Fantasy

Your subconscious, unexpressed needs in relationships may have been reflected in other childhood experiences, such as in the stories and fairy tales that were told or read to you. Many people rely on the big heady feelings experienced in fairy tales, often expecting that they'll always be present. If these feelings aren't experienced within ROCD thinking, you can be sure that checking in with yourself at any given moment will follow.

As Einav says, fairy tales and stories make sense: *"Implicit and explicit expectations about romantic relationships reflect, in part, cultural norms of prototypes of presumably ideal relationships". Einav (2014).*

Many a thesis explores fairy tales in great depth, revealing many layers of psychological meaning. I reference these magical, fairy-dusted tales to enhance your understanding of subconscious ideas of excitement and expectations you might hold for future relationships.

When you consider your current expectation to "live happily ever after", and when you think back to the fairy tales you were once told, how much thought did you give to whether Cinderella wore glass slippers for the rest of her life? Did she and her prince never disagree?

Once upon a time, as a child listening to or watching fairy tales, you probably became immersed in the magic of the story as it unfolded, and you were encouraged by creative thinking; you walked in the character's shoes as if they were your own. This can be stored in your mind as an exciting and desirable experience to look forward to in the future.

6.3 The Impact of Society and Social Media

As indicated in chapter 3, **Relationship OCD**, the use of social media can result in unfavourable comparisons to your relationship, as researched by *The Gottman Institute:*

> *Genesis Games, LMHC, and blogger for The Gottman Institute (2019) says, "People can go above and beyond to curate a perfect feed with the enhanced highlights of their relationship…This is all you see. You don't see the criticisms or the defensiveness. You don't see them crying. You don't see the hard conversations and the vulnerability that accompanies those. You don't see the behind-the-scenes. Yet, you compare your good enough and imperfect relationship to a perfectly curated 'Instagramable' relationship".*

Most people using modern technology subscribe to social media to some extent. Why not, when they're effective platforms for friendships, debate, education, research, marketing forums and promoting business brands and current trends?

Social media marketing company *Smart Insights* recently published its latest media statistics research summary for 2022 *(Dave Chaffey, 2022)*, which states that *"59% of the world's population uses social media. The average daily usage is 2 hours and 29 minutes)."* *(GlobalWebIndex, July 2022)*. Therefore, with the associated hashtags and algorithms, if one click takes you to a relationship resource, your media feeds will soon be influencing and encouraging you to click a bit more around the World Wide Web, fuelling your obsessive thoughts and reassurance seeking and checking compulsions.

Therefore, your internet scrolling can lead you to influencers that allude to relationship goals, such as personality tests, horoscope matching, dating sites and relationship discussion forums. Have you been on any of these and felt instantly disillusioned with what you have or felt heightened into achieving these ideals?

It's easy to ride on the crest of a wave with your surfing, but a note of caution! If you're researching, check that the information is from a reputable site that carries out qualitative research that can be repeated for future studies.

6.4 Entertainment

Just as fairy tales, fantasies and stories create our romantic idealisations, the same can be said for:

- influential blockbuster movies,
- TV programmes,
- reality shows,

- magazine articles,
- TV advertising (for example, for perfume and aftershave),
- poems,
- novels and song lyrics,

No wonder the absorption of all these influences creates comparison and longing and sets high expectations to fit in and be accepted.

"Love is passion, obsessions, someone you can't live without."

– (Meet Joe Black, 1998. American romantic fantasy film)

6.5 Attachment Styles

Attachment theory is applied in many approaches within psychotherapy, counselling and social work.

Did you know?

The research and development of attachment theory have evolved from the work of *John Bowlby (1907-1990)*, a British psychologist and psychiatrist. He explained that early childhood attachment experiences could subconsciously play out in later relationship roles. This theory's further contributions and development were highlighted by the pioneering study *"strange situation"* by American-Canadian psychologist *Mary Ainsworth (1913-1999)*. This study developed a measuring tool designed to assess anxiety, stranger anxiety and the secure base concept of attachment within infants and children.

Attachment theory, therefore, refers to the influences on an infant's/child's development and the sense of security and safety they received from parents/caregivers, described by Bowlby as *"a lasting psychological connectedness between human beings." (Bowlby, 1969).* This was further researched in *Michal Einav*'s work with childhood perceptions.

> *"Attachment is an emotional bond with another person. Bowlby believed that the earliest bonds formed by children with their caregivers have a tremendous impact that continues through life..."*
> *(Verywellmind.com).*

It can be helpful to consider or identify your attachment style and explore alternative reactions to manage relationship difficulties. Your attachment style can influence your coping strategies and behaviours to fulfil your emotional needs and physical connections within your relationships.

Four attachment styles have been identified within this theory and, in their simplest form, are:

- **Secure Attachment**
  As an infant/child, you felt safe, secure, able to be vulnerable, understood and comforted in your emotional connections without a need for reassurance or validation. You built a positive self-image and self-worth. As an adult, you can provide and receive emotional support, trust, believe you're worthy, and make autonomous decisions.
- **Avoidant/Anxious/Disorganised Attachment**
  These three insecure attachment styles formed when your perception as an infant/child was that your emotional or basic needs were not met by your parents/caregivers. Emotional care, support and reassurance were inconsistent, leading to confusion and fear.

'The Attachment Project' has a passion for raising awareness and providing insight to increase people's knowledge and understanding of human attachment. They state that, *"although not necessarily through neglect"*, caregivers *"tend to avoid displaying emotion and intimacy and are often mis-attuned to the child's emotional needs. Such caregivers are reserved and seem to back off when the child reaches out for support, reassurance and affection". (The Attachment Project, Sept 12, 2022)*

These insecure attachment styles can be very debilitating, causing extreme anxiety, insecurity, the need for much reassurance or even self-sabotage in relationships (picking fights, 'testing' a partner, etc.), misinterpretation of conversations and body language and intense feelings of shame and guilt, leading to low self-esteem and self-worth.

6.6 Example of Subconscious Relationship Beliefs

One of my favourite treats is watching period dramas.

You my be familiar with the recent *Netflix* series "Bridgerton", based on the novels by *Julia Quinn*. I hope this isn't a spoiler for those who haven't seen it or have avoided it because of your anticipated trigger reactions. Look away now and skip these paragraphs if you're still holding out for a series binge!

Otherwise, I hope you continue reading, as I think it's a great example of how subconscious beliefs in relationships can be formulated within the above theories.

"Bridgerton" is set in London during the era of elite society, presenting upper-class young ladies to court to be matched with upper-class men for a suitable marriage.

After witnessing the sudden death of his father by a bee sting, one of the leading characters, Anthony, inherits the title of Viscount Bridgerton – and all the accompanying family responsibilities that come with it – at 18 years old.

Anthony is the eldest son of the family. His father also left behind a wholly devastated and about-to-give-birth widow and six other children.

Moving forwards, Anthony meets Kate after much secret lower-class philandering and trying hard to ignore his mother's endeavours to set him up with a suitable bride. He struggles hugely with his emotions for Kate, who also carries 'head of the family' duties for her sister and mother. Whilst Kate is looking to bring about a suitable marriage between her sister and Anthony, she similarly struggles with sacrificing her desires for him.

During the emotional turmoil of his feelings towards Kate and his hesitancy in proposing to her sister, the series reflects on when his father died. It explores the devastating impact on his mother, her very long days of depression, her suicidal ideas and the enormity of what was expected of him from then on.

His interpretation of relationships and his justifications behind his reluctance to marry were countered by his belief that his duty is to his family and their successful futures, thereby forfeiting his own. He copes with his ignored and unsupported emotions, fears and grief by resolving not to allow anyone to endure the devastating position he and his family found themselves in by setting high standards for everything and expecting everyone to get things right. He adopts an arrogant, protective and fastidious persona towards his siblings and relationship needs.

The true feelings he wrestles with become more apparent when Kate is stung by a bee, and his panic resurfaces by reliving his father's death. This pains him enormously because, in his mind, he has a list of criteria for a suitable wife, in a way that would continue to serve his perceived role within his family. He couldn't risk suffering a loss like the one he and his mother had suffered by loving someone.

He was torn between holding himself to ransom and accountable to his earlier, now subconscious, childhood and teenaged beliefs of 'getting it right', 'being perfect', 'not failing', 'being able to cope' and 'being good enough for his family', which included the traditions high-society families followed for courtship and marriage.

You might see how confusing, complex and distressing Anthony found his true, conscious feelings, which conflicted with his subconscious mind.

6.7 Subconscious Relationship Beliefs Exercise

This exercise may help you discover and explore where any potential beliefs and influences you hold around relationships come from and whether they're realistic interpretations and expectations.

> *"Before starting this journey, I believed the unconscious bias to be true and that the thoughts and dreams I experienced were trying to tell me something." (Anonymous client.)*

What automatically comes to mind as 'yes' or 'no' or even 'maybe' answers when you consider each statement? Think about each one rationally and objectively. Recognise the 'should', 'never', 'wrong' and 'always' words I discuss in the later **Core Values** chapter, which suggests rigid inflexibility and extreme terminology leads to anxious and obsessive relationship thoughts.

1. I believe in 'The One'.
2. Love is all about feelings, and they should always be there.
3. I should always feel happy with my partner.
4. It's not ok to feel unhappy with my partner.
5. If I find another person attractive when I'm in a relationship, that means the relationship is wrong.
6. I should never question why I'm with my partner.
7. I should never find my partner annoying.
8. I should never find my partner unattractive.
9. I should never think my partner is unintelligent.
10. I should always feel connected to my partner.
11. My relationship should feel right and be perfect all the time.
12. If we don't agree with each other all the time, then we're not a perfect match.
13. My family and friends should think my relationship is perfect.
14. If I'm in the right relationship, I'll never think or dream of another person or past relationship.
15. I should always want to have sex with my partner at least x times per week.
16. My partner should meet all my needs.
17. I should always miss my partner when we're apart.
18. I should only go to social events with my partner.

19. If we don't have the same interests or hobbies, then the relationship is wrong.
20. My partner should always know what to say and how to behave when I'm down.
21. When my partner and I are together, we should have intense feelings towards each other.
22. I should always want to be with my partner.
23. If I ever feel envious of a single friend's lifestyle, my relationship is wrong.
24. My relationship should be perfect.
25. My partner should be the other half of me; otherwise, the relationship is wrong.
26. My partner should never feel bad because of me.
27. I should always make my partner happy.
28. My partner should always make me happy.
29. I'm responsible for how my partner feels.
30. My partner is responsible for making me feel better.

I'm sure this isn't an exhaustive list of statements you hold, but see if you can rewrite each one that reflects the flexibility needed with human relationships, unintentional mistakes, how much responsibility is placed upon each person in the relationship and whether your relationship generally meets your needs in conjunction with your value system. You might find it helpful to refer to chapter 9, **Core Values**, for this exercise, which includes information on personal boundaries and the ruler scale for flexibility.

As you work through the exercises in this book and record them in your journal, you can constantly revisit these statements and your original answers to see if your perspective is changing.

CHAPTER **7**

Managing Anxiety with ROCD

As you learned earlier, OCD is a common problem, and there are several types (subsets) of OCD, with relationship OCD being one of them. Therefore, there can be a massive variance in the obsessions and compulsions that individuals experience.

You'll also recall that practising exposure and response is considered to achieve high success rates in tolerating the anxiety accompanying your obsessive thoughts in OCD. I also believe this guide's other techniques will help holistically increase self-awareness.

However, before we get to that point, in my experience, many people don't know how to manage anxiety effectively or don't consistently practice managing anxiety regularly – not just for their ROCD, but where life stressors can be experienced at higher levels in general.

Therefore, I find it helpful to incorporate some anxiety management techniques before moving on to exposure and response. Exposure and response can be difficult, and I'm not looking for you to run for the hills before you barely get started on some of the other recommended exercises.

To achieve success, you need the willingness to commit yourself to change and remain motivated. This may mean taking a softer approach initially; however, facing your fears and tackling your thoughts head-on can be hard work, so you might feel like your anxiety is increasing.

Many people mention they've listened to or read about some techniques to manage anxiety. However, they don't familiarise themselves with these techniques, so when they're mid-anxiety, any good intentions go out of the window. Panic ensues, and they feel like they're back at square one. They may feel hopeless, berate themselves further and believe they'll always feel like this, and their self-esteem takes another nose-dive.

I strongly recommend trying them out so you can learn to support yourself by encouraging rational, objective thinking. This can influence healthier, preferred outcomes.

I include four techniques within this self-help guide that I've found particularly helpful. They all work pretty nicely together, or you can use them individually. They're not one-size-fits-all strategies, and there are other valuable resources available on each technique if they don't quite fit for you.

7.1 Breathing Exercises

One of the most well-known and practical exercises to relieve anxiety and stress is to practice proper breathing techniques. Inhaling breath speeds up your heart rate, and exhaling breath slows it down. Changing the proportion of breath inhaled versus exhaled sends messages to your brain to calm the nervous system.

Try practising this exercise below:

- Sit or stand – whichever feels most comfortable.
- Breathe in slowly through your nose to a count of four (or to whatever count comfortably feels like you've filled the space under your rib cage).

- Hold for a moment.
- Exhale slowly through your mouth to a count of six (or to whatever count comfortably feels like you've expelled the air from your lungs).
- Repeat for a couple of minutes at least.

This exercise will help calm your nervous system and enable you to think more rationally.

To get into good breathing practice, I suggest a mindful approach by trying it out, regardless of whether you're experiencing anxiety.

Try the above exercise first thing in the morning, sitting up in bed in readiness for your morning ahead.

Repeat at lunchtime to consciously let go of your morning and prepare for your afternoon.

Repeat when you go to bed to let go of your day in readiness for relaxation.

You'll feel prepared to put your breathing techniques into action whenever you feel anxious.

Following on from this breathing technique, you can move immediately into the following exercise when you're experiencing anxiety. This can give you an added distraction from any emotional distress.

7.2 Grounding Techniques

Grounding techniques can be used against anxiety and panic to enable you to bring mindful attention back to the present and distract from negative emotional disturbances by using your sensory organs. Your five senses are what you can see, hear, touch, taste and smell.

This technique is commonly known as the 5-4-3-2-1 approach, so named because you use your five senses in a way that brings your attention to, for example, five things you can see, four things you can hear, three things you can touch, two things you can taste and one thing you can smell.

A technique I find helpful and a little simpler to remember when experiencing anxiety is finding one personal activity for each sense. I also add a hypnotherapy component to this approach.

This can be a personal, mobile toolbox that you can utilise almost anywhere, and I suggest you prepare for this in advance.

Consider one thing you like for each of your five senses that's personal to you.

For example:

- For taste, you might carry your favourite pack of mints in your pocket.
- For smell, you could use your favourite scent on a tissue.
- For sight, you might choose a favourite magazine you can flick through or a family photograph.
- For sound, you might select a favourite tune from your music list.
- For touch, you might like the feel of a clothing fabric you are wearing.

Once you have your ideas, curl your fingers into a tight ball, clench your hand by your side and remember them. You've captured your toolbox in your hand. This is your anchor (an element from hypnotherapy). In hypnotherapy terms, an anchor is your subconscious automatically triggering a response to your five senses, which can be negative or positive. I'm using this anchor as a positive reminder that you can draw upon your toolbox of favoured five-sense experiences.

Once you've completed your breathing exercise, unclench your hand.

Your attention will automatically be drawn to utilising one or more of your grounding techniques to encourage your mind back to the present.

It's also a great distraction to give your mind space before engaging with thoughts and your usual coping strategies.

7.3 Mindfulness Techniques

To behave mindfully means to bring your awareness to the present moment instead of focusing your attention on the past or the future (magical thinking, predictions or premonitions). It's become a widely recognised and recommended practice, encouraged and supported by health and well-being professionals. Figure 4 highlights how not being mindful and focusing attention on past or future thinking can create anxiety.

In general, learning to become more mindful creates space in your mind to focus on the things you enjoy in life, bringing positive meaning, balance and perspective by recognising positive feelings and emotions.

Mind full vs Mindful

Figure 4 – Being Mindful

Did you know? 💡

The concept of mindfulness originates from Buddhism but doesn't mean being a Buddhist.

Mindfulness encourages you to accept that you live in a life of change and nothing is permanent – noticing how thoughts, feelings and physical sensations feel in your body and being able to observe these thoughts and feelings without attaching meaning and control. Slowing down on immediate reactions to thoughts and feelings can help you respond to them in more helpful and compassionate ways.

Studies into mindfulness-based interventions suggest significant effects in cognitive-based therapeutic approaches, improving mood and reducing maladaptive behaviours by changing an individual's perspective on unpleasant thoughts, feelings and sensations. *(Mindfulness-based interventions for Anxiety and Depression (2017), National Library of Medicine).*

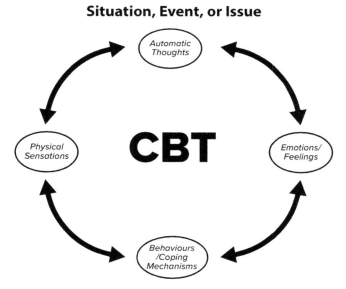

Figure 5 – CBT Subconscious Blueprint

Look at this blueprint again to help you bring awareness to one of your ROCD thoughts in the moment and use it as a guide to see if you're thoughts/internal experiences are appropriate to the actual situation.

Here's an example:

Situation: You're out socially with friends, and the conversation turns to the current cost of living crisis.

Thoughts: What if my partner comes across as unintelligent and doesn't have anything profound to say?

Emotions/Feelings: Embarrassed, worried, fearful.

Behaviour: Talk for or over your partner, make an excuse by saying that some other people want to speak with you and guide your partner away.

Physical Sensations: Anxiety – tummy wobbles, hot and sweaty, palpitations, light headedness, wobbly legs, urge to use the toilet for example.

Consider the effects of the thoughts on how you feel and behave.

From chapter 9, **Core Values** and using the self-compassion exercise within this chapter, what might you say to a friend feeling this way? Might your friend have tried to pre-empt what was going to happen next? How helpful would it be to withdraw from the situation? Could your friend have known what the topic of conversation would be? Is it reasonable to believe that they can control what conversations take place? Is it fair to think their partner's opinion would be unintelligent and the direst consequences would occur?

Compassionately, you might identify that your thoughts are overestimating the threat of a situation. Potentially, you could already have these stored in your mind and be hypervigilant about the whole occasion. Therefore, consider practising mindfulness alongside compassion; otherwise, you could perceive more threat than is necessary to that social occasion (see Figure 4).

There are many ways to practice mindfulness through meditation that you might find helpful. It can take a little time to master, but you may find it helpful through consistent use.

Most people run busy lives, so my preference for an easily accessible mindfulness technique is called *wakeful meditation*, which I learned in my mindfulness training (www.centreofexcellence.com). I've chosen wakeful meditation because you don't need to set aside any specific time to practice in this way. If you already have a mindful or meditative technique that works for you, continue using it and try this one, too, if you like.

Whilst training as a mindfulness practitioner, my attention was brought to the idea that we all carry out many mundane tasks daily. Mundane tasks are repetitive daily activities that you don't need to re-learn each time. Examples include taking a shower, washing your hair, mowing the lawn, peeling the potatoes, washing up, driving to work, walking the dog and vacuuming your home.

Imagine you're doing any of these activities and where your mind might be. The mind can multi-task when it doesn't have to focus on how to do each activity because it already knows, so a variety of thinking expeditions can continue while you're completing these tasks.

When do your ROCD thoughts get in the way of your day? Nearly, if not all, day, forsaking everything else?

7.4 Mindfulness Exercise

Are you taking a shower? Bring your attention to the water on your skin. Is it hot, warm or cool? What does your shower gel lather feel like? Creamy, bubbly, silky? Does your hair 'squeak' when you rinse your hair?

How about walking your dog? How do you even talk to yourself about walking your dog? I changed my internal dialogue to: "The dog and I are going for a walk." What does the temperature outdoors feel like? Can you feel a breeze on your face? What can you see in nature? For example, are there other people you might acknowledge with a "good morning"?

These are just a few examples of routine tasks (mundane or not) that you might carry out daily or weekly.

Practice this technique for a few days when you recognise you're doing a mundane task. You might later choose more appealing times and activities when you can experience the chance to be more present to enhance your general well-being.

Going back to my mindful internal dialogue of "The dog and I are going for a walk" (he does have a name, by the way, rather than 'the dog'!), here are a couple of photos (Figure 6) that I use as my screen saver to remind me of our mindful walk. They're a reminder that I've seen beautiful cloud formations, the colour of the sky and the sea. I've smelt the tide being out and the natural environment. It's better to balance my day rather than be lost in my head with another round of spinning thoughts.

You may feel anxious about leaving the ROCD thought alone, so utilise the breathing exercises and grounding techniques above, which are mindful in themselves.

You can also incorporate the chapter 8, **Fact or Opinion**, exercise. This allows you to give yourself permission to acknowledge, observe and accept that your ROCD thought is there, and you'll look at it a little later if you need to.

Figure 6a – Mindfulness Reminders from My Photo Gallery

Incidentally, by being more mindful of my walk with my dog, my attention was brought to a tree that seemed home to an array of little birds. I named it 'the singing tree'. Even those present moments can be a noticeable memory jogger for mindfulness. Every day I listen out for the singing tree. Passing hello's and making small talk with fellow dog walkers have even made them mindfully aware of the singing tree. I love being able to pass on good vibes!

Figure 6b – Mindfulness Reminders from My Photo Gallery

Figure 7 – The 'Singing Tree'

What activities might you be able to practice being more mindful with?

7.5 Interacting with your 'Security Guard' Exercise

The *amygdala* is the part of the brain that sends and processes information in the *limbic system* (the control centre for the body). It provides emotions such as fear of perceived or actual threats and anger, which triggers the fight or flight response, as explained in chapter 4, **Anxiety.** It also picks up pleasure and produces the same adrenaline and hormones we call excitement. Some food for thought – when you check in to see if the anxiety is still there and think you want to rid yourself of it forever – if you really could rid yourself of anxiety, you'd be ridding yourself of excitement too.

Of course, this explanation is simplified, and much more information is necessary to fully understand how the brain functions. I'm not looking to go too off-grid with the science rather than focusing on overcoming your ROCD.

I aim to keep this guide relatively jargon-free to enable a clear understanding rather than making this a biology lesson. Still, it can be interesting and helpful to have some background information.

Did you know? ☀

German physicist and physician *Hermann von Helmholtz (1821–1894)* significantly contributed to the physics behind sensory physiology. He determined that being consciously aware of sensory information, including thoughts, took up to 35 metres per second. It's now considered that, depending on the factors involved for data to travel through the nervous system, it can take 550–750 milliseconds.

It's pretty quick. No wonder your ROCD thoughts pop up seemingly out of nowhere, and your perceptions, interpretations and reactions are instantaneous. You may have heard of the expressions 'faster than the speed of light' or 'in the blink of an eye'.

In my counselling work, I often use analogies to give a contrast or explanation in everyday language that's user-friendly to help clients understand how things work.

My research on OCD and anxiety through professional development courses from *Wale Oladipo,* Director of Mindbody

Breakthrough Ltd, undoubtedly support this. *Wale Oladipo* is a public mental health coach and psychotherapist. Certified and accredited professional organisations have regulated his training programmes throughout the UK.

He explains that you can interact effectively with your 'manager' (the anxiety – your natural protector) and embrace it as a friend who has your back rather than your enemy. You can decrease anxiety and rumination by focusing on the present with how you communicate with and control your anxiety instead of trying to micro-manage it. Remember, anxiety is the survival instinct that protects you from actual or perceived threats.

Understandably, anxiety can be activated by thoughts and memories of past traumas. Hypervigilant ideas sent to your brain train your mind to be on guard for perceived threats right now and into the future, blowing things out of proportion and often ending with speculative and catastrophic consequences. Modern life pressures, work stressors and relationship issues can increase anxiety, so you remain alert. We can't see inside our heads, so everything can feel like tangled-up wool.

Figure 8 – Detangling the Tangle

The **Security Guard Exercise** below exemplifies how you can effectively lead your 'manager'. Visualise this exercise as a significantly slowed-down version of the amygdala doing its job.

- Imagine that your amygdala is your very own personal security guard. Your security guard has known you all your life and continually looks out for you. It has immediate access to a complete archive of your memories, thoughts and interpretations (including those about your relationship). You can give it a name if you want.

- You're on the ground floor, and your security guard is on the tenth floor.

- You have a worrying, intrusive thought that you send (at the speed of light) to your security guard, who senses imminent or perceived danger. Your security guard processes this as fear, sending your nervous system a shot of adrenaline and accompanying chemicals and hormones in readiness for your fight or flight response.

- You *feel* this uncomfortable physical sensation and call it anxiety.

- Your security guard is waiting to see what you'll do next. In all probability, and in response to the physical symptoms you're experiencing, you send up another worrying thought, something like, "that means (insert negative consequence)". Your security guard sends another shot of adrenaline in response, so your anxiety increases.

- You make sense of this thought and accompanying anxiety as further validation there's something in this thought that requires further investigation. Your thoughts become more rapidly obsessive, searching for the answer, the certainty, the guarantees, resulting in the compulsions of checking, reassurance seeking, micro-managing, avoiding, etc.

- Once you've gone around the emotional washing machine cycle, you reach the inevitable and only conclusion available to you – that you're going to leave the relationship.

- Whilst the emotional washing machine cycle is taking place, your security guard has alerted your other brain functions to make sense of all these possible clues within your thought process (imagine these other brain functions are the rest of your security staff).
- The rest of the security staff also hold all the information they know about you – your core beliefs, interpretations, memories, images, feelings, needs and coping strategies. This information is potentially outdated or a gross misrepresentation of who you are and your needs. They're referring to all that old stuff, much like an out-of-date work CV that only highlights your childhood paper round.
- Equally, that decision to leave the relationship is a message to your security guard – a strong message – that states what you'll do. Your security guard doesn't need to send you another shot of adrenaline.
- Your anxiety calms.
- You experience temporary relief, but it's short-lived because the conscious, rational and objective part of your mind gets an opportunity to participate in the discussion, and you don't want the relationship to end. Your partner, rationally, fulfils many of your hopes and ideals in a partner. Of course, they're not perfect; who is? Of course, you may have the odd disagreement or difference of opinion; who doesn't?
- What happens next?
- You send your security guard more doubting thoughts about your decision, and the whole process starts again (emotional washing machine).

As referenced in chapter 4, **Anxiety**, your security guard (the amygdala) is your natural protector.

Your security guard <u>accepts</u> everything you tell it. It doesn't have a filter to determine true or false thoughts.

Therefore, I strongly encourage you to use your core values (chapter 9) as your frame of reference to support you in making conscious decisions based on your hopes, dreams, desires and passions and the boundaries you place on them. They're much more realistic and consider the bigger picture, unlike anxiety, which is a less stable indicator, as it's isolated to your train of thought at the time of your ROCD spiral.

For this exercise, practice acknowledging and appreciating the alert and send a message that you're not in immediate danger at the first opportunity. You're looking to embrace your security guard as your best friend who'll always have your back. It may sometimes misfire, so being mindful and using breathing and grounding techniques will support you. Using the **Fact or Opinion** exercise in chapter 8 to encourage balance, you can also permit yourself to postpone the thought.

An example of your security guard having a misfire and working for you at the speed of light might look a little like this:

You're in the yoghurt section of your local supermarket, minding your own business and deciding what flavours you might like for lunch that week. You hear "BOO!" right in your ear. Immediately, your whole body's reflexes are startled into a jump. This is your security guard alerting you to threats. You spin around, only to see that it's Bill from accounts that you chat to at the coffee machine. In a millisecond, your visual senses send a message to your security guard that it's Bill playing silly tricks on you before you even utter an expletive word at him for giving you such a fright. Your security guard acknowledges your decision that Bill is no threat and doesn't send you an adrenaline shot, and your body recovers to its normal state.

Alternatively, you might realise that the loud noise you react to might not be Bill as you swing around. You might send your security guard a "What was that loud noise?" followed up with "I hope it's not a bomb," (two thoughts), in which case, your security guard will continue to follow up your thinking with shots of adrenaline until you make sense of the situation. In reality, the tinned baked bean tower was too tall and fell over. Thankfully, nobody was injured.

Acknowledging and appreciating your security guard may feel difficult initially. Still, you're building a new range of coping strategies, unlike the old, familiarly comfortable (but equally uncomfortable) method of the past. Consistent practice will start to feel more natural while your brain continually receives up-to-date information about you. You'll be managing your anxiety rather than it controlling you.

Many people state they get anxious about getting anxious.

Let go of the grip of anxiety by understanding that your security guard knows their job inside and out. Its actions will lessen with the up-to-date information you give it. You don't need to pay your security guard overtime by draining your emotions and depleting your self-esteem, self-worth and valuable time.

Of course, as I mentioned earlier, the thoughts can pop up at the speed of light, so it will take some practice to start catching them.

CHAPTER **8**

Fact or Opinion?

Many people believe that if a thought or thoughts continually pop up around their relationship and are causing a great deal of anxiety, it's their gut – something from deep within – telling them their thoughts are the truth.

These 'facts' become intrusive and worrying, making it increasingly difficult to resist paying attention to them.

Professor Paul Salkovskis, Programme Director for the Doctorate in Clinical Psychology at the *Oxford Institute,* is commended with extensive journals and research into OCD, explaining that many people will experience intrusive thoughts. However, people with OCD believe that thinking about something is the same as actually doing it or that it *will* happen, and they put actions in place to prevent it. This is called *thought-action fusion*, commonly called *magical thinking.*

When you start thinking this way, you've placed your thoughts as a priority in your mind, giving them meaning and importance, creating a sense of urgency to find an answer so you can lessen the anxiety and distress you're now experiencing. You really feel that you *need* that answer!

"A wandering thought about what it would be like to be unfaithful to a partner does not make you seek an affair."

– (Winston, 2017. Overcoming Unwanted Intrusive Thoughts).

From chapter 3, **Relationship OCD**, you'll recall Figure 2 and how I referred to it as an *emotional washing machine.* You have the thought, which brings about a feeling/emotion that re-intensifies your feelings/emotions, so a vicious cycle commences.

You convince yourself that the anxiety will disappear if you can find an answer. Consider the following questions. Does your anxiety reduce the more you question it? Does your anxiety reduce even more when accompanied by your 'what if...' style questions?

How often have you tried to ignore or avoid your relationship thoughts only to find they come back repeatedly, thus increasing your anxiety and other negative feelings and emotions?

How often have you thought they MUST be true because the same persistent thoughts keep coming back?

How often have you believed that if a thought is persistent and *as you had the thought in the first place*, its intrusive, worrying content will inevitably become true or happen anyway?

How often have you contemplated past experiences within your relationships in search of clues about the validity of the thought?

How often have you told yourself you're a terrible person for having these thoughts?

How often have you carried out actions to cope with your fear of the thoughts being valid, only to find they return repeatedly?

Consider Figure 9. You'll notice that questioning your thoughts this way serves no purpose in finding a conclusive answer but results in the opposite effect – increasing your anxiety.

Magical thinking styles don't mean that perceived events in the future are facts, nor do they determine your character, personality, sense of identity or intention.

The co-authors of *"Overcoming Unwanted Intrusive Thoughts"* *(Winston and Seif,* 2014) concur: *"The fact is that a thought is not a message about what will happen. Similarly, a thought is not a prediction or warning of an awful action or occurrence in the future…it is not an accurate reading of the future".*

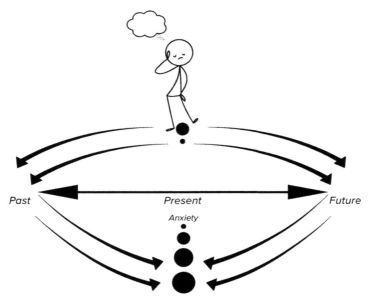

Figure 9 – Rumination and Magical Thinking

The circles represent the stages of your anxiety. Notice a little anxiety to start with. Whichever way you work with it, ruminating over past experiences with your partner – or even previous relationships – brings you to the present with increased anxiety, which makes you peer into the future using your magical thinking and then returns you to the present, which increases your stress. Unfortunately, you don't have the capabilities to change any 'evidence' from the past, and neither do you have a crystal ball to predict the future.

What happens with this style of overthinking is you hope that if you can work out the future, you'll find the answers to your thoughts and know what actions to take in the present; therefore, your anxiety will subside. You prepare yourself!

Ruminating about the past is unhelpful because your internal voice sends you messages that criticise, belittle and bully you for not having had the sense to know the early warning signs. This lowers your self-esteem and leaves you feeling unable to make good decisions for yourself (hence creating your checking and reassurance-seeking behaviours, which attempt to tackle the problem).

This means you're not in the here and now, leaving you feeling disconnected from your partner and relationship.

However, in various ways, your ruminating internal 'worried' voice continually tries *"to argue, control, avoid, suppress, reassure, reason with, neutralise, or work around whatever thoughts come up for you." (Winston, 2017)*.

Try the below exercise using the techniques offered in chapter 7, **Managing Anxiety with ROCD.** It gives you a flavour of how to begin accepting and observing your ROCD thoughts without immediately engaging with them, using the concept of acceptance and commitment therapy.

8.1 Fact or Opinion Exercise

This exercise requires you to allocate a 15 to 20-minute self-reflective period at the end of your day when you've done everything you need to, but not before bedtime. That is not a time to self-reflect when you want to relax for the night!

I explained how the 'emotional washing machine' works in chapter 3, **Relationship OCD.** When you engage so urgently with your thoughts that they become entangled, it becomes doubtful that any rational or objective thinking can occur.

You are looking to postpone the thought(s). By doing this, you're providing some distance from and acknowledging the thought(s), but you're also managing and tolerating the anxiety that comes with them. Consistent practice will disengage you from the fear. You're not attempting to avoid or ignore your thoughts but instead permitting yourself to look at them later in the day.

This exercise isn't designed to find conclusive answers to your thoughts or questions but to help you manage them more effectively by providing balance. This is achieved by challenging the thoughts or questions with something you know as FACTUAL EVIDENCE about the situation or your partner. Equally, it is not to be confused with neutralisation attempts to avoid or ignore your thoughts or behaviours.

All the new coping strategies discussed in this guide fit seamlessly once you understand their purpose and have mastered them individually. You won't always have to set time aside for daily self-reflection. Your subconscious will eventually learn these techniques so that you carry them out more naturally and in the moment.

So, you've chosen the time of your self-reflective period. This might be 7 pm.

Whenever you experience an ROCD thought, remind yourself you're permitting the thought to occur, mentally wrap it up in cotton wool and put it on a shelf in your mind. You're looking to do this with kindness. You can write it down or mentally recall it during your self-reflective period. Do that with each thought. YES, it's likely to feel challenging and anxiety-provoking, so I suggest you use the techniques in the **Managing Anxiety with ROCD** chapter as the softer approach to exposure and response exercises.

Once it's 7 pm, recall your thoughts or pieces of paper. If they no longer are causing any emotional distress, mentally discard it as one not to consider. It doesn't matter if the thought returns another day or if you recognise it as a recurring thought – you always have the next day to address it.

For each thought, what do you know, or what have you evidenced during your relationship that might dispute its truth? For example, "I don't think my partner's funny enough". Has your partner NEVER made you laugh, told a joke or provided humour in your relationship? Write down some examples that you can recall. You don't need to write down the whole life span of the relationship, just three or four examples to balance and challenge the negative thought(s).

You might also recognise that your thoughts or opinions lead to distressing feelings/emotions, reinforcing the next thought. They re-intensify or bring on further negative feelings, and so forth. Hence, the emotional washing machine occurs, and any factual or evidence-based information is omitted.

Should you be concerned about the word "enough"? Do you know how to quantify it? This word frequently pops up without any clear ideas of what it might represent. Most dictionary definitions and synonyms state 'enough' as being 'sufficient' or 'adequate for the intended purpose'.

Repeat this every day until you're familiar enough to carry it out mentally.

CHAPTER **9**

Core Values

What are core values?

A research paper written by Daniela Kirova (2021) for The Values Institute states that *"Core values serve as criteria or standards, guiding the choice or evaluation of people, actions or events."*(An excerpt from her overview of *Shalom H. Schwartz, Theory of Basic Values, 1992).*

Core values are essential in establishing a good sense of worth and will help you understand your own identity – an identity you like and love.

"Empower yourself using your values with intention."

This chapter includes an exercise that's one of the most important to carry out.

You'll recall that one of the three themes I find commonly presents itself in ROCD is a low sense of self-worth, which relates to your value system and self-esteem.

In chapter 7, **Managing Anxiety with ROCD**, I shared how my clients use their physical symptoms of anxiety as a gauge/measuring tool to validate or authenticate their relationship thoughts or situations.

By determining what you stand for – your morals, principles, virtues and the values you hold dear – you can switch from using anxiety as your measuring tool to this much more helpful strategy. You'll find an increased sense of purpose to problem-solve, remain in the present, look at ways to reach the goals you seek and engage in meaningful and helpful communication. You can shift away from the coping strategy of rumination.

It's a significant boost to your self-awareness, as ordinarily, you don't walk around with an advertising board over your shoulders stating what you stand for. Equally, you probably don't give too much consideration to your values other than just accepting who you are, whether you like or dislike these aspects of yourself.

This makes sense, as many of our core values are deeply ingrained, given to us by our parents/caregivers and other significant people from a young age.

Life messages or proverbs attached to these values can appear in generations of families, society and culture and are explicitly said or implied. This also applies to your interpretation of the content and implication of these values from all sources and can be internalised as your sense of self and value.

Some relationship messages or proverbs might sound like this:

"If you aren't married by X age, nobody will want you, and you'll be a spinster/bachelor forever."

"You made your bed; you lie in it."

"Play the field while you can."

"Tied to the ball and chain."

"The grass is (or isn't) always greener on the other side."

"There are plenty more fish in the sea."

"And they all lived happily ever after."

"Watch out for the seven-year itch."

"All's fair in love and war."

"A chip off the old block."

"The apple doesn't fall far from the tree."

In your journal, record some life messages that might have influenced your thoughts and feelings.

I mentioned 'values' briefly in chapter 6, **Subconscious Relationship Beliefs and Requirements**. Life experiences increase as we get older, and undoubtedly, the influence of society's values plays a part in how we experience ourselves in areas like relationships, success, wealth, happiness, health, fitness, body size, security, etc., as well as opinions, our environment, and the evolution of trends. It's easy to assume that if society dictates what we 'should' be doing, then we should be doing it. This can often create an uncomfortable disconnect between these 'should be doing' things and fulfilling your needs.

In my generation, a perceived social value towards relationships was to meet your ideal partner and get down the aisle damn quickly. Otherwise, you'd be 'left on the shelf' (another life message/proverb). Starting a family early was also desirable. A house, mortgage, and an excellent job signified success (a societal value to measure your worth against).

You might recognise many 'shoulds' or 'shouldn'ts' in your internal dialogue. In my counselling training, my tutors described this as *shouldisms*.

These might be thoughts such as: "I should be happy with my partner all of the time", "I shouldn't be thinking like this about my partner", "I shouldn't keep checking my partner for flaws" or "we should look good together", for example.

See how that translates in your rigid thinking too: "If I'm not happy with my partner all the time, then the relationship is *wrong*" or "I'm *wrong* for checking my partner for flaws". There are many examples of us saying they or I *should*, which easily translates into "They (or I) are *wrong*" in the context of the message you're giving yourself.

This is another example of using critical self-talk, which can hit your self-esteem and increase anxiety, misrepresenting your worth and value as a whole person.

It's a very rigid terminology, with no flexibility or recognition that you're holding yourself to ransom, and again bullying, criticising and belittling yourself with little or no compassion. Therefore, you might recognise how easy it is to use anxiety as a measuring tool to validate your thoughts.

"How do I forgive myself for having these thoughts about my partner or relationship now or ever?" (Anonymous client)

Think self-compassion.

Critical judgement of your ROCD thoughts results in a lack of self-compassion. Once you recognise your lack of self-compassion towards your ROCD thoughts, you might also become aware of hijacking self-compassion in other situations with harsh and judgemental thoughts and behaviours.

Compassion is ordinarily a standard that most people hold as a personal value and is usually thought of as 'having compassion for another person', but it can be majorly lacking in application to themselves. We'll move on to that in the self-compassion exercises to help you care for yourself more kindly.

When we think of the people we meet in our life, maybe friends and work colleagues, we instinctively know if we like them without questioning why in too much detail.

I suggest it's because they generally represent traits we have in ourselves – our core values, morals and principles – which help us choose the relationships we engage in.

I say 'generally', as we might favour some values in people more than others when considering how an individual enhances our life and how our principles align with fulfilling our needs.

Let me give you an example of how someone might refer to their core values as a guideline to help them in just one part of a situation. This is not attached to a romantic relationship:

Sarah's had a terrible day at work. She's had several recently and feels overwhelmed, unappreciated for all the overtime she's undertaken, and very tired. She feels like a failure and like she's not good enough. She's been managing a staff team, and staffing levels have been at an undesirable minimum due to reasons outside of her control, such as staff sickness and already booked holidays. She's recently passed a business exam, which formed one of the requirements for her promotion to manager. However, her current experiences have left her ruminating on a time she lost a job when a company felt she wasn't ready for the role's responsibilities. She notices she's creating an assumption in her mind that this will be a repeat performance.

Ordinarily, she's the life and soul of many a party. She's confident and enjoys dancing the night away, packing her free time with social events with friends and family. Her self-esteem has taken a hit, and she wants to share her experience with someone and talk it out.

Sarah has three terrific friends: Tania, Molly and Rebecca.

Tania also likes to party and accepts as many invitations as possible to socialise. She's an animal lover and loves the outdoors and action-packed holidays. She appeals to some of Sarah's high-priority values of having fun and adventure, her sensitive, caring nature to animals and people and her sense of spontaneity.

Molly is full of confidence with her knowledge of I.T. She can be outspoken and hold firm opinions about what is fair and just. She organises and plans to minute detail. She's a highflyer in the technological world. Molly appeals to some of Sarah's high-priority values of self-confidence, fairness, justice and determination within her work ethos.

Rebecca is a nurse. She works under extreme pressure and is tirelessly empathetic, level-headed and kind. Rebecca rides horses with Sarah at the weekend, and they sometimes camp in nearby woodlands. They enjoy the solitude and peace after a hard day mucking out the horses and tending to haybales. Rebecca appeals to some of Sarah's high-priority values of kindness, compassion, patience and love for animals. Sarah appreciates and respects Rebecca's compassion for others and how she extends compassion to her self-care.

All three friends bring value to Sarah's life, and all four have enjoyed holidays and nights out and share a high work ethic.

In Sarah's *current* situation, she's experiencing a hit on her self-esteem.

She draws upon her core values to guide and explore what she might need to help her tend to and sit with her upsetting thoughts and emotions. They can help her evaluate her problems, respond to them more objectively and rationally in relation to her sense of value and worth, and lead her to make autonomous decisions.

Sarah is self-aware and recognises that her current thoughts, emotions and feelings attached to this situation affect her self-esteem and don't determine her whole sense of identity (self-worth). In the section about self-worth and self-esteem, you'll recall that, although they are closely related, they're not the same.

Although all three friends provide value in her life, she chooses Rebecca to call upon. She's not looking to go horse riding and doesn't need medical attention, but she recognises her need for compassion, patience and space to talk things through and gather her thoughts. She's not looking for opinions or reassurance but respects Rebecca for managing her self-care in tranquil environments to collect her personal thoughts.

Using your core values as your frame of reference instead of your anxiety levels will lead you to meet your present needs and solve problems more efficiently.

Additionally, Sarah choosing Rebecca is separate from *reassurance seeking,* as reassurance seeking from others diminishes your confidence in your decision-making. It may temporarily decrease your anxiety if someone agrees with you. Still, it doesn't serve as a long-term benefit and reinforces your belief to rely on another person's judgement rather than your own, provides only temporary solace and can lead to avoidance of experiencing your own emotions and feelings. Understanding your core values encourages you to validate yourself instead of relying on external validation. Of course, there's nothing wrong with asking for the opinions of others, as they can provide other options to consider along with your own and can help you gain perspective in many situations.

Whilst experiencing an ROCD spiral of intrusive, worrying, doubtful, upsetting, uncertain and anxiety-driven thoughts, I recognise the draw towards reassurance seeking and checking behaviours towards partners to see if they fulfil any needs/expectations (or all of them) in the moment.

Peterson & Seligman's (2004) research into character strengths states, *"The display of a strength by one person does not diminish those surrounding him or her"*. They also say that *"It must manifest in a way that can be assessed, and at least somewhat stable across time and situations."*

The point I'm making is that, within ROCD, *everything* you value about yourself, your partner and your relationship is questioned, in its entirety, in the heat of the moment. There's an urgency to answering ROCD thoughts in terms of the value of the relationship. However, it's unrealistic to expect certainty and guarantees (hence the compulsions). Imagine a box of chocolates, taking one and not liking that particular flavour, then deciding you don't or won't like the whole box and discarding it! (I don't think I could do that with a box of chocolates!

These obsessive thoughts focus on the *whole* relationship in minute detail and increase anxiety. Hence, the state of anxiety is used as a measuring tool for the suitability of the entire relationship, based on ONE situation. Another example of thinking this way is, "is my partner funny enough?" – how much is 'enough', and when is it appropriate to be 'funny'? Would you want your partner to be funny 24/7? How might that appeal to you if that value were inappropriate, and you'd like your partner to express care for you? This is what ROCD does – it distorts the whole picture.

In Sarah's situation, she drew on her core values to explore what she needed *at the time*, although all three of her friends provided value and worth in her life.

Another example of attempting to problem-solve life worries by using anxiety as the measuring tool instead of a personal value system might look like this:

Robert's considering looking for a new job. His thoughts go like this:

"I'd like to leave this job and get a new one."
"What if I leave and can't get a new one?"
"What if I never get a job again?"
"Maybe I'd better stay where I am."
"I'm not good enough for a new job."
"I'll stay where I am, then."
"What if my whole team resign, though?"
"Maybe they all hate me?"
"I'm not very good at this job."
- *"Look at what happened when I had to remind Darren about his working hours when he kept turning up late."*
- *"He hates me. That's why he didn't tell me about his personal problems."*
- *"I upset him."*
- *"I should be able to recognise if someone in my team is unhappy."*

- *"What did I miss?"*
- *"I was wrong to mention it to him when I didn't know the problem."*
- *"When word gets around about how horrible I was to him, the rest of the team will definitely leave."*
- *"I'm not good enough."*
- *"I think I'll probably lose my job."*
- *"Maybe I should resign?"*
- *"What if I don't ever get another job?"*

A relationship OCD thinking spiral might go like this:

"That person's attractive."
"What does that mean?"
"Would I rather be with that person?"
"I feel really ashamed/guilty thinking like this."
"What would my partner think of me?"
"Maybe I should tell my partner."
"I feel really bad."
"This must mean I want to be with that person, and they're a better fit."
"If I walk past that person now, that means I want to pursue them."
"What if they make eye contact, and I look back?"
"I might smile back…that just proves it."
"I'll walk the other way!"

This thought process is gathering momentum and increasing anxiety, like the emotional washing machine. The decision to 'walk the other way' lessens the anxiety, as you've given your *security guard* a decision. However, the decision is driven by anxiety that the thoughts are true.

If you chose to refer to your core value system, you might have recognised that, even if you thought the person was attractive, it doesn't mean you intend to follow through with anything that supports your thoughts as being realistic.

This thought process could lead to further ideas of what you might do, increasing anxiety levels again.

Your values incorporate your moral standing, virtues and principles. These apply to decisions you can make about everything, including your relationships. Using your core values provides a more stable reference guide, and you can learn to trust that you can make good decisions for yourself.

Obsessive thoughts driven by anxiety happen rapidly and can lead to catastrophic consequences, leaving no space for rational and objective thinking, no space for any factual evidence that these thoughts might not be true and bringing feelings of 'stuck-ness', limiting your potential and self-worth.

Over the years, I've gathered many resources to support people in overcoming ROCD that work well with each of the three identified themes – anxiety, OCD (obsessive thoughts and associated compulsions) and self-worth/self-esteem.

Everyone can feel anxious to varying degrees towards many situations in life and will, in all probability, experience it again due to its natural human state.

"I think one of the things that were crucial in my understanding of the work and what I was expecting out of ROCD therapy was when I asked you what being 'recovered' looked like,

and you said that it wasn't having no anxiety or doubt, because for a long time I kept looking for the feelings of uncertainty to go away, for me to be 100% sure and suddenly anxiety free."
– Anonymous client.

How you experience your sense of self can often be impacted negatively, leaving you feeling uncertain and somewhat shaky at times.

The following exercise in core values isn't designed to eliminate anxiety (because it can't). Still, I believe it can go a long way in helping you make decisions that are right for you, raise your self-confidence and empower you.

For every resource I've found for the ROCD exercises, I've ascertained their effectiveness by practising them myself and through client feedback. This is my favourite, as I mentioned earlier.

It's helped me recognise that my whole worth or value isn't based solely on some anxiety-provoking life experiences. It's also a helpful reminder to balance the negative and the positive.

Personal values provide an internal reference for what is good, beneficial, important, useful, beautiful, desirable, and constructive. Values are one of the factors that generate behaviour (besides needs, interests, and habits) and influence the choices made by an individual. (Wikipedia [ethics and social sciences]).

9.1 Core Values Exercise

Using your journal:

1. From your perspective, write down three or four core values that you feel your parents/caregivers have, or people that were close to you as a child.
2. Consider the content of these values and how each person demonstrates them.
3. Think of three or four values that someone you respect or admire has. This can be someone you know or don't know or several people.
4. Consider how you feel this person/these people demonstrate these values. You may or may not have these values yourself, but you can if you want to!
5. Write down three or more values that you feel society holds generally.
6. Consider the values you feel society holds based on your gender and age. This is important because, on reflection at the end of this exercise, it will help you explore any influences or interpretations you may have because of them.
7. Repeat step three, considering the values you feel society holds, particularly concerning romantic relationships, based on your gender and age.
8. Write a list of core values you would *like* to have yourself. You can have as many as you'd like, not just three or four, as in the steps above. To help you, there's a list of words at the back of the book that may consist of values, virtues and principles. Feel free to add any of your own.
9. Put your words into priority order and choose your top ten (or a few more if you like).

Your top ten (or more) are the ones you want to focus on. Explore how these values might show up in your life – how you demonstrate them to others and yourself!

The remaining values are important but may have more desirability than *essentiality* and *consistency.*

What do I mean by *desirability?* If you've ever applied for a job and received a job description, usually, there's a person specification accompanying it. A person specification helps you see, at a glance, the qualities a company's looking for in a person for the job role, e.g. qualifications, experience and knowledge. It will also state how the person can demonstrate these descriptors, indicating whether they're *essential* or *desirable.* The *essentials* are necessary or important for the applicant to hold. The *desirables* are worthwhile or useful to have but aren't essential.

Thinking of your core values list this way may help you decide if you have a little wiggle room to give them.

In general, your top ten might not need to be so rigidly in place that there's no room for manoeuvre (unless it's a value/moral code that absolutely mustn't be crossed; we all have some of them). Everyone needs a little tolerance. Otherwise, we're prone to inflexibility, shouldisms and potentially unrealistic, high expectations. But equally, your values need boundaries.

At the end of this exercise, I'll explain a method called the 'ruler scale' to support you with tolerance and managing the 'shoulds' more effectively in a way that doesn't cross the personal boundaries of your core values.

Considering steps 1-9 above, from your perspective, what are the values you *live* by?

Consider the parental/caregiving values you may have been influenced by (these may be deeply ingrained) and the societal values that have led you to doubt your decisions and compare them to others. The values you're living by may, of course, include ones you would actually like.

If you refer to the example I gave of the *Netflix* series *Bridgerton*, you may recognise the family and societal values by which Anthony Bridgerton was heavily influenced. That's not to say they were wrong or unwanted, but they could've been adjusted and updated (as Anthony Bridgerton did in the end) or thrown out altogether if he'd wanted.

You can decide on the core values you want throughout your life's journey. You can also UPDATE them when you choose or RE-PRIORITISE.

For example, a value of mine is about family. My parents both have family values. Some of my mother's family values showed up as the nurture and care of my siblings and myself. She also carried out the domestic chores and cleaning (I imagine, within the agreed balance of my parent's relationship and the influence of social norms within their generation). On the other hand, my father demonstrated his family values as the main financial provider, working long hours (in line with his strong work ethic) and returning from work with dinner prepared and on the table and the children ready for bed.

Although my family values are ingrained, I recognise – through self-reflective personal development – that my parents' demonstrations of this value were replicated in my younger years. No consideration was given to generational and environmental changes, including the difference in available opportunities and my own needs. I've since updated my values to incorporate content I want to include or discount. For example, I have a strong work ethic from my father that I'm proud of, as it's taught me to learn freely, be independent and provide for my own family. This has been adjusted over the years, as my own (now adult) children no longer need the same level of nurturing as they did as young children, so my role has changed

Identifying and establishing your core values will help you develop your self-awareness, help you recognise your needs and guide your behaviours and decision-making on life's journey.

a little. My work ethic can increase, as I have more time to spend on my passion for counselling. This offers me more flexibility and adaptability than the 'shoulds', without discounting them altogether. They've become more user-friendly.

The same concept can be applied to society's values. Quite often, women mention to me that society values beauty. Many trends come and go, so it can be difficult and anxiety-provoking if you feel pressured to conform rigidly to some of society's values. This can attack your self-esteem and self-worth. Still, we can choose preferences without feeling squeezed into a corner. What comes to my mind in societal trends at the moment for women, in particular, is eyebrow shaping and lip enhancements. What comes to your mind that you feel influenced by or that you should be conforming to?

Figure 10 – Your Core Values Will Guide You on Life's Journey

It's worth remembering that your core values can be adjusted and amended.

As life evolves and responsibilities change, check in on your core values as a reference for yourself to see if they're still in alignment with your goals and direction in life. Imagine it as a mental health CV. Questioning yourself leads to healthy decision-making based on values.

ROCD thinking can lend itself to spending time ruminating on past relationships and comparing them to new ones. Could your needs have changed in conjunction with your values? What you were looking for or had ten years ago might be different from what you want now. ROCD-style of thinking isn't about whether long-term relationships stand the test of time or how they grow together.

9.2 Self-Compassion

What is self-compassion?

Compassion comes from the Latin word *compati* and means 'to suffer with'.

The leading research by *Dr Kristin Neff,* Associate Professor of Educational Psychology at the University of Texas, Austin, informs the **self-compassion** exercises in this book. With her empirical research and training for teachers worldwide, she's a pioneer in self-compassion. Many therapists support her work within their own.

She reminds you that part of being human means that, along life's journey, things don't always go as you want them to. You'll experience frustrations, mistakes and losses –a reality that faces us all.

Her research encompasses three elements of what self-compassion is versus what it's not:

Self-kindness vs. Self-judgement

A calm presence of mind with warmth, understanding and gentleness when life experiences are complex or challenging, and an acceptance of the reality that people can't always be, or get, precisely what they want, versus anger towards themselves, frustration and critical self-talk.

Common Humanity vs. Isolation

When experiencing levels of anger, frustration and criticism towards themselves, a person can often feel isolated, like they're the only one suffering. Self-compassion recognises that these human experiences can be suffered by anyone (because people are mortal, vulnerable and imperfect); therefore, they're not alone.

Mindfulness vs. Over-identification

Adopting a mindful approach to thoughts and feelings entails being non-judgemental and observing them as they are in the moment rather than attempting to ignore them, push them away or refuse them. Being mindful helps give balance and perspective to thoughts and feelings instead of over-identifying them as being your whole self.

"With self-compassion, we give ourselves the same kindness and care we'd give to a good friend."
– (Neff, 2015).

9.3 Self-compassion Exercise

To hold compassion for another person means recognising their suffering and responding with warmth, understanding, kindness and care, and without judgement.

1. Think of your best friend, a loved family member or someone very close to you.
2. You may consider someone who approached you in the past, or you might imagine the person is experiencing a level of emotional distress towards their circumstances. How would you 'be' in this situation? Can you imagine what you might say to them? *How* might you speak to them? Write it out on a piece of paper if you like.
3. Secondly, imagine how you respond to your ROCD thoughts. Are you judging yourself and the situation harshly? Are you reacting to your thoughts in a critical and bullying way? You can write out a scenario for yourself.
4. Compare the two situations. Can you recognise a difference?

Neff also states that your tone of voice can influence how you view yourself. Does your internal voice sound caring, warm, understanding, kind and non-judgemental? Probably not.

Many theorists refer to this voice as your *internal critical voice*. It's precisely what it says on the tin – critical, judgemental, harsh and usually unhelpful. In all probability, you wouldn't turn round to your friend and agree with them that yes, they are stupid and always do stupid things, or say, "yes, you should be upset/mad for having these thoughts or allowing this situation to happen", while speaking to them in a cross and aggressive manner! If you were to, you'd show little understanding, support and compassion. Talking to yourself like this sounds like you're heaping on a lot more emotional distress and kicking yourself when you're already down! There's further information on where your inner critical voice takes you in chapter 10, **Internal Critical Voice and Comparison**, along with some ideas to develop more positive thought strategies.

Therefore, developing self-compassion is something I enthusiastically ask you to practice. To embrace the three components of self-compassion for what they are rather than what they aren't, think about how you might offer yourself the same level of compassion as you would that dear friend.

Work on catching up with yourself as soon as you recognise a spiral of ROCD thoughts.

What might you need RIGHT NOW?

What would be a level of kindness you could offer yourself in the moment?

If you're labelling yourself as 'stupid', might you tell your friend that they're not stupid and remind them of times they haven't been stupid?

Are you holding yourself accountable to such an extent that you feel very alone, like you're the only person who's ever felt bad about themselves?

Can you offer yourself some self-care, draw upon your values as Sarah did in the previous example and call upon a friend who supports you if you feel caught up in a negative cycle (not for reassurance purposes but for *understanding*)?

Can you bring your attention to your voice and say the above things in a warmer tone?

When you focus on this internal voice, you might also recognise that you identify yourself with these harsh judgements.

Imagine you had a day that involved a visit to your GP – your internal voice is saying you're anxious about visiting the GP, you're always forgetful and you're just plain stupid.

After that, you're hosting a work presentation for people you don't know – your internal voice is saying you're anxious about hosting the work presentation because you're just not good enough and people will see through you.

After the work presentation, you're catching a train to an unfamiliar destination – your internal voice says you're anxious about catching the train. You always need to depend on others to feel secure.

See how you might be identifying yourself as an anxious person. Remember, anxiety is your fight, flight, freeze or fawn response.

Consider challenging yourself with the word 'anxiety' and be more probing about the thinking behind it.

Changing your wording when reflecting on your internal dialogue might help you to discover you're concerned about the GP visit because you recall that previous visits have left you forgetting some of the information you wanted to ask for, which has led to criticisms of yourself 'for always being forgetful'. This discovery could lead you to problem-solve and write down what you want to ask this time, making you less anxious. After all, if you check this against your value system, you might recognise that you're not always forgetful, as you don't forget to do tasks at work or ordinarily miss appointments.

You might not know the people at the work presentation, but you might be worried that your work 'isn't good enough'. You might reflect on how much research you carried out, the work you've put into it and that you've given it your best shot because this presentation is important to you.

You might not have travelled on a train for a long time, so you might check the timetable for potential changes and where the next platform is in preparation, rather than bullying yourself out of it and saying that 'you can't travel alone'. You might recognise that your value system is proud of your independence.

9.4 Personal Boundaries

What are they, and why are they important?

In the workplace, you'll have many policies to guide and advise you on achieving the best possible standards, objectives and outcomes – boundaries being included within these.

Your boundaries are connected to the core values, principles, virtues and moral standing you hold for yourself, which determine your self-worth.

What people can often do in their personal life is neglect these boundaries and become 'yes' people (people-pleasing), causing anxiety in themselves and lowering their self-esteem. From chapter 4, **Anxiety**, you'll recognise *pleasing* as the *fawn* response.

Some feelings, such as guilt, anger and resentment, might mean you're waiving your rights to personal boundaries for someone else. Or perhaps your limits have blurred along the way, leaving you feeling worn out and preoccupied to the detriment of your own life needs and those who are important to you.

Setting personal boundaries doesn't mean you become selfish; you become assertive, confident and self-aware, keep your unique identity intact and encourage healthy mental well-being. Personal boundaries protect you from being manipulated and taken advantage of. It means that you have the same respect for your boundaries as for your employer's, friend's or family's, and you have the right to expect other people to respect yours.

How do you think, feel and behave, and what physical symptoms do you experience when you're around someone crossing your boundaries? Your limitations are probably crossed if you feel all-consumed or uncomfortable with yourself around that person or situation.

Write a list of your preferences for how you'd like to be treated by others. What's ok and what's not ok? How are you feeling? Why? What would you like to do? Why are you feeling guilt or stress? Compare these alongside the **Core Values** exercise you've just carried out in conjunction with the values you actually live your life by.

9.5 The 'Ruler Scale' Exercise

When you chose your value system in the **Core Values** exercise, you identified your top ten(ish) – the essentials that show up consistently in how you manage your life and your reference point to guide you towards your hopes and dreams, desires and passions (although we don't ALWAYS get what we want!). Therefore, good connections and relationships with others can be made when they display similar traits to you, AND you can also recognise that some values are desirable rather than essential.

ROCD thoughts around expectations and feelings are very rigid and relatively inflexible!

Personal boundaries attached to your values are essential. However, inflexibility can be unhelpful and lead you straight back to the 'shoulds'.

Equally, there's no flexibility when engaging in reassurance and checking behaviours alongside these thoughts. This **Ruler Scale** exercise may help you offer yourself some elbow room without compromising your values or crossing your boundaries. (You can also refer to this scale for the **Reducing Checking and Reassurance-Seeking Behaviours** exercise later in chapter 13).

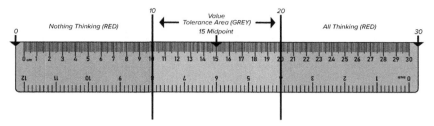

Figure 11 – The 'Ruler Scale'

'All or nothing' or 'black and white' thinking styles make up much of your ROCD thoughts.

The thought of the 'grey area' is somewhat disturbing for most due to uncertainty and its lack of absolute answers. This scale is designed to embrace the grey area as being within the realms of regularity.

In chapter 3, **Relationship OCD**, there were examples of inflexibility, certainties and guarantees you're searching for to find your answer. To offer a little flexibility without flouting your values and boundaries, *consistently*, *in general* or *most of the time* might be more effective terminology (after all, it's the human condition sometimes to make mistakes without intention).

Imagine that 0 on the ruler scale represents the 'nothing' thinking (here, you probably wouldn't care about your relationship and wouldn't be reading this book or even be in the relationship).

Imagine that 30 on the ruler scale represents the 'all' thinking (a high expectation that your partner SHOULD invoke highly intense feelings in you every time you think of them, or you SHOULD find them attractive, intelligent etc., at the very moment of the thought).

Your aim within ROCD thinking has been 30!

Shift that scale down to 15 – this is your mid-point. Your *'consistently'*, *'in general'* and *'usually'* words. Consider this an excellent place to be.

From that mid-point, shift the scale down to 10 and repeat it the other way to 20 (this is only for illustrative purposes to understand flexibility; you don't have to give your *in general* such a wide berth!).

The area between 10 and 20 is your grey zone, with 15 as your mid-point.

The areas between 0 and 10, and 20 and 30 represent your red zones (negative or positive).

If your ROCD thought was questioning your level of attractiveness to your partner, in the moment, can you determine that you *consistently* never find them attractive, and therefore you're constantly in the red zone, even when your rational and objective thoughts suggest otherwise?

If your ROCD thought was suggesting your partner's no fun, are they ALWAYS no fun, have NEVER been fun, and it MUST mean they're going to be boring FOREVER, and therefore the relationship is wrong?

Using the ruler scale allows you to determine the *consistency*, *in general* or *usually* terminology in conjunction with the values you hold, realistic expectations within the relationship or the value the relationship brings to your life. The grey zone offers a comfortable place to be, allowing for a bit of tolerance for *occasional* moments. Still, sometimes you might creep into red zones.

Imagine you went for a meal out at your favourite restaurant. This restaurant brings good value – ambience, location, service, price and food quality. On this occasion, the usual chef is on holiday, and they have a replacement. Your food is not quite up to the standard you expect, so your mid-point slides towards 10. However, all the other contingents that make up this meal are still of good value, so you will probably return. That uses the ruler scale to highlight whether the content of your thoughts slides into the negative red zone all the time or once in a while and helps you decide if those moments are tolerable.

Moving the other way from 20 to 30 is also a red zone, but for positive thoughts.

Re-using the restaurant visit as an example, imagine the replacement chef cooks something that delights your taste buds more than usual. You've gone into the red zone, but positively. However, the replacement chef isn't there the next time you return, and the regular chef cooks to a consistent standard that you're happy with.

The above examples show that once in a while, your experiences might slide into negative or positive incidents. They might occasionally even be an 'ouch' moment, which might not indicate an absolute red flag or that a catastrophic outcome is inevitable.

Chapter **10**

Inner Critical Voice and Comparison

The previous chapter, **Core Values**, spoke of self-compassion and what it is versus what it's not.

10.1 What is your Inner Critical Voice?

It's exactly how it reads. Within your relationships (as well as other areas of your life), it leads you to doubt, question and distrust your desires, hopes and dreams. Your inner critical voice consists of thoughts that use extreme terminologies, like "I will never...", "My life will always be...", "I can't handle this relationship stress," and "I'd be better off alone". It harbours old beliefs and ideas you have about yourself and others that only serve to lower your self-esteem further, leading to the even more extreme statements of "I'm useless", "I'm worthless", "I feel hopeless" and "I feel helpless".

This critical thinking style originates from earlier life experiences that led you to make interpretations about yourself that then play out in later life. These interpretations are often untrue. Chapter 2, **Cognitive Behaviour Therapy (CBT)**, explained this further as part of the negative core belief system that can become deeply ingrained, putting further limitations on your desires, hopes and dreams.

When you experience low self-esteem, as you can see, the examples above show words that end in '*less*'. 'Less than'. When you

"Comparison is the crush of conformity from one side and competition from the other – it's trying to simultaneously fit in and stand out. Comparison says, 'Be like everyone else, but better.'"
– (Brene Brown, 2021).

start describing yourself as *less than others*, this is where *unfavourable comparison* steps in.

10.2 Comparison

Comparison can be viewed as positive and negative.

A comparison could be used more as an adjective like *'comparative'*, meaning there is little or no difference to a situation, thing or person. It's *equal.*

Additionally, comparison to something or someone else might be seen as positive in terms of the feelings and beliefs it generates within you. It could indicate something you want to work towards as a result of respect and admiration, and you feel able to work on adopting the strategies for yourself. For example, the **Core Values** exercise explores how you might admire or respect another person's values as something you feel is reasonable to achieve for yourself.

Unfavourable comparisons can harm your mental well-being, leading to negative feelings like guilt, envy, resentment, fear, anger, sadness and even depression. Unfavourable comparison leaves you feeling inferior (less than), leading to low self-esteem and self-worth, impacting how you view your future.

You'll recall that social media can significantly influence the unfavourable comparison you experience when you only see a snapshot of someone else's life. Remember, many people only portray what they want the world to see – you don't see the 'perfect couple's' anguish and arguing over which selfie, out of many, they'll post when posing for the perfect picture and angle.

If you recognise that you spend much time googling and comparing your relationship to influences on social platforms, consider limiting the time you spend scrolling and shift your attention to more mindful activities you can practice. Add in some gratitude (things you're thankful for) to balance the unfavourable comparison.

Earlier this year, I decided to become a little fitter and exercise more. Off the back of my newfound activities, the exercise trainer always ended the sessions by suggesting that I think of three things I might be grateful for today. It made me realise how easy it is to focus on the negative and pay very little attention to the things that bring me joy and what I'm thankful for. Try it out; it doesn't have to be materialistic things. You might surprise yourself – I rarely come up with the same gratitude list daily.

10.3 Moving away from the inner critical voice

Your inner critical voice will attack you amid an ROCD spiral of thinking. Bringing your attention to your thoughts – either through journaling or making a conscious effort to note your tone of voice and the words you use to describe the situation or yourself – can help you learn to adjust them, so they become more reasonable. Your inner critical voice also influences your behaviour, leading to avoidance or reassurance seeking and checking tendencies associated with ROCD.

Figure 12 – Inner Critical Voice and Comparison

For example, if you're focusing on unfavourable comparisons, remind yourself of your strengths and qualities. Amend extreme "I always" and "I never" styles of thinking by responding with something that challenges what the comparison is saying to you. The **Core Values** exercise will help you shift your attention to your positive self-worth, so you can respond with encouragement rather than criticism. Be kind to your feelings, and don't take responsibility for everything. Focus on being 'good enough' for yourself and others – perfection is setting too high a standard, and you wouldn't rationally expect others to be perfect all the time. Refer to the exercise in chapter 9 **Core Values** on **Compassion**. If you try to walk through life on a tightrope of perfection, you'll eventually fall off, so work on forgiving yourself for any mistakes. It's called being human. Your inner critical voice holds you to ransom, holds no compassion and is a manipulative bully.

CHAPTER **11**

Creating an Exposure and Response Hierarchy

It's normal to want to avoid or check out feared situations, as it creates very uncomfortable feelings and emotions. In OCD and ROCD, these emotions are intensely heightened.

A technique within CBT is to introduce a hierarchy of feared and anxiety-driven situations in gradual steps.

As you've learned, the compulsions in ROCD maintain the anxious thoughts, providing only temporary relief before the whole emotional washing machine cycle starts again.

Using the exercises in this book, I hope you've gained some understanding of the thoughts/beliefs and compulsions that maintain your ROCD and that you feel ready to commit to tolerating the anxiety by starting the process of exposure and response. I hope you've gained a level of perspective, so you're prepared to experience more happiness and peace of mind in your life.

You control this process; you choose the exposure, starting with a minor, anxiety-provoking trigger. This will take some time as you repeat the exposure until the anxiety has disappeared, working your way up to the most fear-inducing trigger, but it will be worth it. In my experience, it has a drip-feed effect in that the more difficult triggers naturally become less difficult with your growing confidence and increased self-esteem in combatting your anxiety. The following **Theory A versus Theory B** exercise will guide you, as well as the **Reducing Reassurance and Checking Behaviours** exercise, as it's similar but worded differently to help you explore alternative perspectives.

It isn't easy; however, *OCD-UK* states, *"Generally, people find that exposure exercises are not as difficult as they thought they would be and their anxiety and fears fade away much quicker than they ever imagined"*. This can, in part, be due to the CBT element of a step-by-step approach to the exposures and the more in-depth understanding of your behaviours linked to outdated subconscious core beliefs, rather than earlier versions of exposure and response therapy where the person was thrown in the deep end.

At the beginning of the book, you'll recall that I brought your attention to three identified themes of ROCD that may also be prevalent in other areas of your life and your relationship. As a reminder, these were anxiety, OCD and self-esteem/self-worth. Before starting the previous exercises we examined a structured CBT approach of activities as a gentler path to reach your goal.

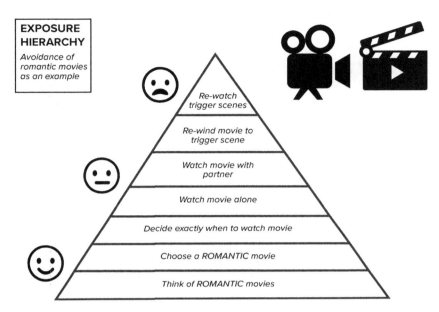

Figure 13 – Exposure Hierarchy

It's all about perspective.

What do you see? A rabbit, duck or both?

Ludwig Wittgenstein's work in philosophical investigations made this rabbit-duck illusion famous. Psychologist Joseph Jastrow and others used it as a means of demonstrating two different ways of seeing the same thing.

I'm not for one moment suggesting that a rabbit or duck is threatening, but it's purely a means for alternative interpretation for the following **Theory A versus Theory B** and **Reducing Reassurance & Checking Behaviours** exercises.

Figure 14 – Duck or Rabbit, Duck/Rabbit or Rabbit/Duck

CHAPTER 12

Theory A Versus Theory B Exercise

Theory A versus Theory B is a widely used CBT technique to help people with OCD consider comparing two theories regarding their thoughts. It can be helpful as an exploration of the possibilities of, or alternatives to, ways of thinking that might be more realistic.

Theory A versus Theory B also helps people understand their world. People hold on to beliefs that can sometimes be inaccurate, leading to unhelpful behaviours that reinforce the original thought.

"The most effective way of changing a misinterpretation...is to help the person come up with an alternative, less threatening interpretation of his or her experience."
– (Salkovskis, 1996).

This book's exercises will support you in considering and changing a misinterpretation that you might hold within your ROCD thoughts.

Theory A can be carried out before or during the other exercises in this book. You can then pay attention to Theory B once you've completed the activities and have gained insight and understanding of Theory A's obsessions and compulsions that maintain the problem.

12.1 Theory A

Theory A describes how you view your ROCD problem in further detail. You might want to refer to the earlier distressing thoughts mentioned in the **Introduction** or chapter 3, **Relationship OCD**, including any of your additional ideas that result in what you feel is the only outcome available.

To help guide you in journaling your experiences, consider these questions and add further detail that's important to you:

- Identify your main problem. This may look like, "I have real concerns that my relationship is wrong".
- What might your evidence be to support this way of thinking?
- What are you doing, or what do you think you need to do, if you have real concerns that your relationship is wrong? I.e., what are you paying particular attention to? If you're worrying about unsatisfactory outcomes arising from future events, what actions are you taking to avoid this?
- What do you think about yourself as a person?
- How do you think other people describe you or think about you?
- If all of Theory A is true, how do you feel this will affect your future if you maintain these ROCD thoughts and behaviours and hold firm in your beliefs about yourself?

12.2 Theory B

To gain further insight and perspective, here are some questions to consider. I recommend leaving this exercise at least until you've completed the **Fact or Opinion** exercise in chapter 8, contemplated the **Subconscious Relationship Beliefs and Requirements statements** in chapter 6 and carried out the **Core Values** exercise in chapter 9.

- With your enlightened self-awareness and understanding, what might be another way of thinking about your original problem?
- How might you describe yourself now that aligns with your value system? That might sound like, "I'm a person that cares a lot about my relationships with others, and I also value myself. However, I'm not solely responsible for other people's feelings. They're also adults who can make their own decisions".
- Elaborate on your description of yourself in a journaling exercise.
- Could Theory B be more realistic considering this new evidence and understanding?
- How might you test whether Theory B stands up for itself? Make good use of your sense of identity (self-worth/value) and mindful thinking when reconnecting with your personal goals.
- Are there some things you can tolerate within your relationship that don't cross the personal boundaries of your values?
- What effect might this new thinking have on your current relationship (or future relationships if you're not currently in one)?

The Exposure and Response Hierarchy is designed to help you plan alternative responses to your trigger thoughts instead of relying on the safety behaviours, which are your compulsions. The **Reducing Checking and Reassurance-Seeking Behaviours Exercise** in chapter 13 is also similar.

CHAPTER **13**

Reducing Checking and Reassurance-Seeking Behaviours

In the **Introduction** to ROCD, and recognising it as 'a thing', you might have noticed common thinking styles you adopt that result in checking out your thoughts with their accompanying behaviours and seeking reassurance from other people or other means. The sneakiness of OCD will use every trick in the book to keep you in the vicious cycle of your emotional washing machine, maintaining your obsessive thoughts and compulsions. It can even delude others into unintentionally maintaining the cycle – even as a therapist, I recognised a long time ago that I unintentionally reassured a client by responding to an OCD compulsion via an email when they were emotionally distressed.

Reassurance seeking is typical behaviour for OCD sufferers. It's normal in many situations to ask for assurances that offer an affirmation or level of certainty in relation to things you already deem true from someone else. Reassurance in OCD, however, is repetitive, providing temporary relief from the intrusive and worrying thoughts before the same opinion or different intrusive and worrying relationship thoughts arise again. Those all-too-familiar doubts occur in a vicious cycle.

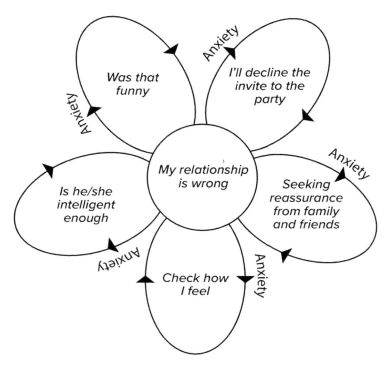

Figure 15 – A Vicious Cycle

Checking behaviours are similar to reassurance seeking, such as testing whether you're experiencing a level of attraction at any given moment or chasing a certain feeling if the thought comes from a worrying, concerned and anxious place. It's almost impossible to manufacture a positive feeling or emotion from negative thinking.

A positive thought generates a positive reaction. A negative thought causes a negative response unless you can determine a rationale based on objectivity and balance based on the bigger picture. Although your anxiety has been temporarily relieved by gaining reassurance from someone else, it doesn't give you full autonomy for your own decisions.

Confessing and apologising can also be forms of seeking reassurance, hoping that your partner or other people might relieve you of your anxiety and the accompanying feelings such as guilt, shame and embarrassment. However, your partner and other people you seek reassurance from don't necessarily recognise this as an OCD compulsion. Although their comfort or kind words help to relieve your anxiety temporarily, it's not long before the cycle starts again.

A constant need for approval, reassurance and acceptance devalues your worth when looking for external validation. Review the **Introduction** and mentions of self-worth and self-esteem to recognise this as one of the three identified themes in ROCD and that you're seeking external validation rather than self-validating. The **Core Values** activity can also help you build a healthier sense of self.

Not all ROCD sufferers have shared their OCD with their partners, friends or family, but if you have, it's worth asking them not to indulge your OCD   in this way and explain that you recognise it only exacerbates your OCD. They might gently be able to point you in the direction of working with your new coping strategies instead.

Exploring the advantages and disadvantages of your current ROCD thoughts and behaviours can help you ascertain how helpful they are in coming up with an alternative theory (chapter 12, **Theory A Versus Theory B**).

It can feel risky to change compulsions that you otherwise believed have kept you safe.

13.1 Reducing Reassurance Seeking & Checking Behaviours Exercise

Now that you've worked with earlier exercises in this book, you can carry out this exercise in your journal with each ROCD thought or behaviour to evaluate its effectiveness:

- Consider each one of your thoughts and behaviours.
- What might be the advantages of engaging with this thought or action?
- What's the outcome you're looking for?
- Are there any disadvantages to this thought or action?
- Does it help you come to a conclusive answer?
- Are the disadvantages outweighing the advantages?
- Alternatively, you might feel there are advantages and disadvantages. Is there another way to look at the problem?
- Can you consider postponing carrying out whatever it is you do?
- Would you like to stop doing it altogether? If that feels difficult, could you do it less?
- From your newly developing self-awareness, do you feel you might be chasing a feeling based on an anxiety-driven thought?
- Are there any facts that challenge the thought?
- Is there another way of thinking or an alternative behaviour you might adopt? Can you use a mindfulness technique you've found helpful to postpone a behaviour?

This exercise in exposure and response is a gentle introduction to purposefully facing anxiety and the uncomfortable emotions it can elicit head on, but you're always in control.

- Write down some new ideas and commit yourself to trying them out. I suggest you start with the one that feels the least anxiety-provoking.
- Once you have your ideas, what might you consider the advantages of this new thought or behaviour?
- What might the disadvantages be?

- How will you manage your anxiety? Which techniques from chapter 7, **Managing Anxiety with ROCD**, have been helpful?
- How will self-compassion support you?
- Once you've journaled or asked yourself these questions, when will you try it out?
- Remember to be specific in your goal plan. Where, when, what and how much time will you spend on trying out your new behaviour?

If you feel anxious about trying something new, compassionately remind yourself that you don't need to bully or criticise yourself. Keep that inner critical voice in check. You want to be your finest champion and best friend (they don't belittle others for effort!). Your security guard will feel more settled when you tell it you've decided.

So, now you've decided to try your new thought or behaviour out.

Of course, trying out something new is challenging and probably will bring about anxiety (even just from thinking about it). Remember, you're committing yourself to change because how you feel has been detrimental to your relationship, consuming your days and evenings and disrupting your sleep. Of course, it might feel scary, but this is an exercise. Be kind to yourself.

Once you've tried it out, take some time to evaluate how it went.

- What happened?
- What did you discover about yourself?
- How did managing your anxiety work out?
- Were there any benefits or disadvantages to the new thought or behaviour?

Suppose it was tough to carry out the new behaviour. In that case, you can consider breaking the new behaviour down into smaller goals and reducing the time spent on your old behaviours, i.e., "I usually spend ten minutes checking if my partner is being humorous in our social circle". Permit yourself to only check for eight minutes, then seven, then six and so forth, using a grounding technique or other distraction until the anxiety lessens to a minimal and manageable level before you move on to further reduced timeframes.

This exercise will bring about longer-term benefits or eliminate the excessive reassurance and checking symptoms altogether. It's essential, as continuing the behaviour only keeps the intrusive thought or behaviour alive. Reassurance seeking and checking behaviours are compulsions.

It can feel risky to change compulsions that you otherwise believe have kept you feeling safe. Even though safety behaviours don't bring about long-term comfortable outcomes, it can feel safer to be uncomfortable with familiar, tried and tested actions.

"Whatever makes you uncomfortable is your biggest opportunity for growth."
– (McGill, 2021. Voice of Reason).

CHAPTER 14

Understanding and Dealing with Common Emotions within ROCD

Guilt, shame and embarrassment are the most common emotions within ROCD that I've come across that people attribute to their intrusive, unwanted and obsessive thoughts towards themselves, their partners and their relationships. All three feelings hurt self-image.

14.1 Guilt

*Definition of **guilt** (noun): a feeling of worry or unhappiness because you've done something wrong, such as causing harm to another person.*

> ***Example:*** *"She remembered with a pang of guilt that she hadn't called her mother."(Cambridge Dictionary).*

14.2 Shame

*Definition of **shame** (noun): an uncomfortable feeling of guilt or being ashamed, because of your or someone else's bad behaviour (loss of honour and respect).*

Example: "He thinks there's a great shame in being out of work and unable to provide for his family." (Cambridge Dictionary).

14.3 Embarrassment

*Definition of **embarrassment** (noun): a feeling of self-consciousness, shame or awkwardness.*

Example: "Nobody spoke for at least five minutes, and Rachel squirmed in her seat in embarrassment." (Cambridge Dictionary).

We can look at guilt in two different ways that interlock with shame.

Guilt is a natural emotion and can be viewed as a positive and healthy response leading to personal growth and responsibility. It can be a helpful indicator that we've gone against the grain of what we morally stand for, as in our value system. We then endeavour to put right a particular wrongdoing. It holds us accountable to our sense of identity – our self-worth. The guilt in the example above is a healthy guilt resulting from breaking a promise she made to herself or her mother based on her moral compass.

Guilt within ROCD intrusive thoughts also holds you accountable, but to the inner critical voice that condemns and judges you into shaming yourself as a wholly 'bad person', meaning the whole you, your whole identity. You may follow this up with additional thoughts or actions to neutralise or apologise for it, which undermines your self-worth.

Intrusive thoughts cause guilt because of the meaning that gets attached to them. They become facts in your mind. The intrusive thoughts become obsessive, which is why you conduct specific actions repeatedly to check and reassure yourself of their truthfulness. They cause high anxiety levels, and the ROCD cycle continues frequently.

Shame can be secretive, leading to perfectionist behaviours in relation to yourself and others because of the guilt you're experiencing. Shame often comes from your inner critical voice, leading you to believe others are better than you and diminishing your self-worth. See the example above that refers to a gentleman who felt ashamed of his whole self because he was out of work, which goes against his work ethos and family values; it sounds like this is out of his control and isn't his intention.

Feelings of embarrassment can be experienced when we feel threatened that our thoughts and feelings, realistic or not, will be recognised by others and that they'll judge us negatively. This is further impacted by physical responses to embarrassment like blushing, stammering, steering a conversation away from a particular topic, etc.

The **Self-Compassion** and **Fact or Opinion** exercises can help you, alongside your values, to pay intrusive thoughts less attention because you have no intention towards them. Practice being kind to yourself next time you experience guilt and shame, and be *curious*. I like to use the word *curious* about your thoughts; it's a gentler and less intimidating way than being critical towards yourself to consider whether your thoughts are helpful and whether your behaviours are rational or irrational responses to situations.

> *"The difference between shame and guilt is the difference between 'I am bad' and 'I did something bad'." – (Brown, 2013. Shame vs. Guilt).*

14.4 Disassociation

Feeling disconnected to present moments is a subconscious, temporary *avoidance* coping mechanism, often described as *disassociation*. Disassociation in anxiety disorders like OCD is defined as an extreme stress or trauma response. People can experience disassociation in several ways – feeling detached from their thoughts, emotions, memory, perception and sense of identity. Ordinarily, these cognitions all work together, but when experiencing disassociation, it feels ruptured. It's like watching yourself in a movie but not feeling like it's you. Other symptoms are described, such as brain fog (having awareness but not feeling anything), feeling like you're on autopilot, having an out-of-body experience and memory loss (not remembering how you might have got to some place, even though you know you are there). *(www.psychcentral. com, March 11, 2022) and (www.upjourney.com, March 16, 2021).*

At *Verywellmind.com, Tull (August 24, 2022)* reported that disassociation is a general term in the context of anxiety disorders.

To manage disassociation-related symptoms, grounding techniques and regular sleep and exercise routines are effective strategies. Grounding techniques can be found in the earlier **Managing Anxiety with ROCD** chapter.

14.5 Grief

Grieving the loss of hopes and dreams in a relationship can understandably be difficult to accept, especially if you've been holding on tight to those relationship hopes for an exceptionally long time. They may have even been built up over years of childhood fantasies and fairy tales – your very own 'and we both lived happily ever after'. Grief isn't only attributed to death; it can accompany the loss of many things, including hopes and dreams.

If you feel very alone with this type of grief, it can sometimes be referred to as *disenfranchised grief*. The suffering you're experiencing isn't necessarily recognised, acknowledged or considered necessary by others, thus increasing the emotions of loneliness, guilt and shame accompanying this type of grief. It can also lead you to minimise your feelings and question your grief's legitimacy.

Disenfranchised Grief – *"Grief that person's experience when they incur a loss that is not or cannot be openly acknowledged, socially sanctioned or publicly mourned."* – *(Doka, 2001).*

As an ROCD sufferer working through this book, you may have experienced grief for all the high-end emotions, sparks, and wonderment you constantly held in high esteem throughout your relationship (or whatever you were working towards). Harbouring your ideas of a relationship can also be a personal experience – maybe not shared with others, but equally, having the belief that others automatically feel the same. It can be a crushing and painful blow to accept what you might now see as realistic versus unrealistic in your current relationship or the experiences of previous relationships. Practice self-compassion with your grief now that you understand where it's come from, and this will help you gently move forward with your core values within a relationship. Give yourself some space to face your emotions without criticism or judgements by conducting compassionate journaling and being kind to your feelings. Guidance from chapter 6, **Subconscious Relationship Beliefs and Requirements**, and the **Self-Compassion** exercise in chapter 9, **Core Values**, will help you.

CHAPTER 15

Core Value Word List

This list of words can assist you in building your core values (refer to chapter 9, **Core Values**). It's not the easiest of tasks once you apply yourself to it, as we rarely consciously consider our values within a daily review. You can choose as many as you like, but you're looking to focus on your top ten (or more, as suggested in the **Core Values** exercise). Using too few limits your individuality and uniqueness, but too many can leave you with too much to focus on. You're looking to see what you truly value as the essence of what's most important to you. The others are still important, and as the **Core Value** exercise suggests, they might be helpful or beneficial, but they're not necessary.

You can group some words into a category and use them in other value groups or leave them as stand-alone words. For example, one of my top priority values is authenticity. If someone were to ask me what that meant, I'd explain that my content within authenticity shows up as being straightforward, honest, open, transparent, etc.

- Accountability
- Achievement
- Adaptability
- Adventure
- Authenticity
- Authority

- Autonomy
- Balance
- Beauty
- Boldness
- Compassion
- Challenge
- Citizenship
- Community
- Competency
- Contribution
- Creativity
- Culture
- Curiosity
- Determination
- Diversity
- Enthusiasm
- Equality
- Ethical
- Fairness
- Faith
- Fame
- Flexible
- Friendships
- Fun
- Growth
- Happiness
- Honesty
- Humour
- Influence
- Ingenuity

- Inner Harmony
- Intellect
- Innovative
- Justice
- Kindness
- Knowledge
- Leadership
- Learning
- Love
- Loyalty
- Meaningful work
- Openness
- Optimism
- Peace
- Persistence
- Pleasure
- Poise
- Popularity
- Recognition
- Reliability
- Religion
- Reputation
- Respect
- Responsibility
- Security
- Self-respect
- Service
- Spirituality
- Stability
- Success

- Status
- Trustworthiness
- Validation
- Wealth
- Wisdom
- Work ethic

This list might not have everything you consider valuable, so feel free to add your own.

Chapter 16

Final Reflections on Your Working Journal

Now that you're coming to the end of this book, here are some questions to consider in your journal:

- How do you feel you've been getting on?
- What have you learned?
- How are you feeling?
- Are you able to manage anxiety more effectively?
- What progress have you made?
- Have you practised anything from an alternative perspective?
- Are there some areas that are more difficult than others?
- What's working well?
- Do you still have concerns in a particular area?
- Which exercises or activities have been helpful?
- Are you finding more space in your day and your mind that used to be filled with obsessive thoughts and compulsions?
- What are you doing to fill that space?
- Have you recognised values that you hold, which are essential, that might fill that space – hobbies, interests, education, work, an adventure, for example?

- Can you use any of the exercises or activities to problem-solve future anxieties?
- From your perspective, how might you continue with positive development? We can all have the odd moment that catches us unawares.

We can all experience anxiety.

It's your alert system that's designed to protect you.

Think of self-compassion when these moments arise in situations that cause a negative emotional impact.

Use your journal to reflect on and add to your progress.

You can revisit any of the exercises whenever you like.

CHAPTER **17**

Final Reflections from Me

So, you've now recognised that relationship OCD is 'a thing'.

You understand how and why OCD can manifest in relationships and how it manipulates your thinking.

You can recognise how subconscious core beliefs about yourself and your relationships can impact your adult relationships.

You can recognise a sense of self that you love.

You can recognise your individuality and uniqueness.

The exercises and activities have equipped you with lots of resources to create a new tool kit to support overcoming your ROCD.

You can measure your progress by reflecting on your journal entries for the activities and exercises.

Your self-compassion supports your deeper self-awareness.

You have a healthier perspective towards healthy relationships and empower yourself.

I hope working through this book has helped you find effective coping strategies for managing anxiety in your relationship and other areas of your life. If the going gets tough, you now have the resources to support you.

Finally, remember to show yourself compassion. After all, if a loved one or friend of yours was suffering, that's precisely what you'd show them.

I wish you great success with your ongoing journey.

Tracy

References

Bowlby, J. (1969). *Attachment. Attachment and loss: Vol. 1. Loss.* P-194. Hogarth Press.

Brown, B. (2021). *Atlas of the heart: Mapping meaningful connection and the language of human experience. Vermilion.*

Rhimes, S. (Executive Producer). (2022). *Bridgerton.* (TV Series). Shondaland.

Cambridge University Press. (n.d.). Shame. In Cambridge Dictionary. Retrieved March 7, 2023, from https://dictionary.cambridge.org/english/shame

Cambridge University Press. (n.d.). Guilt. In Cambridge Dictionary. Retrieved March 7, 2023, from https://dictionary.cambridge.org/english/guilt

Cambridge University Press. (n.d.). Embarrassment. In Cambridge Dictionary. Retrieved March 7, 2023, from https://dictionary.cambridge.org/english/embarrassment

Socratic questioning. (2022, September 22). In *Wikipedia.* https://en.wikipedia.org/wiki/Socratic_questioning

Doka, K.J. (2001). *Disenfranchised grief: New directions, challenges and strategies for practice. Research Press Publishers.*

Neff, K. (2011). *Self-compassion: The proven power of being kind to yourself (10th Anniv. Edition). Yellow Kite.* www.self-compassion.org Dr. Kristin Neff

Neff, K. *Definition of Self-compassion:* Self-Compassion. https:// Definition and Three Elements of Self Compassion | Kristin Neff (self-compassion.org)

Veale, D., & Willson, R.(2009). *Overcoming obsessive compulsive disorder.* Robinson.

Salkovskis, P.M. (1985). Obsessional compulsive problems: A cognitive-behavioural analysis. *Behaviour Research and Therapy, 23(5), 571-583.* https://pubmed.ncbi.nlm.nih.gov/4051930

The Journal of Psychology. (July 2014). Einav, M. *Perception about parents' relationship and parenting quality, attachment styles and young adults' intimate expectations: A cluster analytic approach. Page 2. https://www.researchgate.net/publication/263295975*

Winston, S.M., & Seif, M.N. (2017). Overcoming unwanted intrusive thoughts: A CBT-based guide to getting over frightening, obsessive, or disturbing thoughts. Page 6. New Harbinger.

Kirova, D. (2021, February 23). *What are core values, and why are they important?* www.values.institute/values.

Peterson, C., & Seligman, M.E.P. (2004). *Character strengths and virtues: A handbook and classification.* American Psychological Association; Oxford University Press.

www.attachmentprojection/attachmentstyles/September 12, 2022 – The Attachment Project

G, Games, LMHC. (2019). The Impact of Social Media on Relationships. The Gottman Institute. https://www.gottman.com/blog/the-impact-of-social-media-on-relationships/

Doomscrolling. (2023, February 8). In *Wikipedia.* https://en.wikipedia.org/wiki/Doomscrolling

Value (ethics and social sciences). (2023, March 3). In *Wikipedia.* https://en.wikipedia.org/wiki/Value_(ethics_and_social_sciences)

Centre for Clinical Interventions. *Reducing Reassurance & Checking Behaviours* www.cci.health.wa.gov.au

References

Mindfulness Practitioner www.centreofexcellence.com

www.ncbi.nlm.nih.gov/pmc/articles/PMC5679245 – National Library of Medicine

OCD UK. *The History of OCD. https://www.ocduk.org/ocd/history-of-ocd/*

Disassociation. K, Bettino. March 11, 2022. https://psychcentral.com/what-disassociation-feels-like

Ainsworth, M. (1971-1978). *Strange Situation.* www.simplypsychology.org/mary-ainsworth

Chaffey, D. (August 22, 2022). *Social Media Marketing.* Smart Insights

https:/smartinsights.com/social-media-marketing/social-media-strategy/new-gobal-social-media-research

Core Values. https://www.therapistaid.com/worksheets

Pirri, Traci W. MSW,LCSW, (March 16, 2021). *Disassociation.* www.upjourney.com

Cherry, K. (22 February, 2023). *What Is Attachment Theory? The Importance of Early Emotional Bonds.* https://www.verywellmind.com/what-is-attachment-theory-2795337#toc-attachment-styles

Tull, M. PhD. (August 24, 2022). *What is Dissociation?* https://www.verywellmind.com/dissociation-279292

Printed in Great Britain
by Amazon

23503785R00088